David Rabe's

An Early History of Fire

A Samuel French Acting Edition

SAMUELFRENCH.COM
SAMUELFRENCH-LONDON.CO.UK

Copyright © 2013 by David Rabe. All Rights Reserved.
Cover Art by Rogers Eckersley Design

AN EARLY HISTORY OF FIRE is fully protected under the copyright laws of the United States of America, the British Commonwealth, including Canada, and all other countries of the Copyright Union. All rights, including professional and amateur stage productions, recitation, lecturing, public reading, motion picture, radio broadcasting, television and the rights of translation into foreign languages are strictly reserved.

ISBN **978-0-573-70108-5**

Samuel French
45 West 25th Street
New York, NY 10010

www.SamuelFrench.com

Samuel French
52 Fitzroy Street
London W1T 5JR

www.SamuelFrench-London.co.uk

FOR PRODUCTION INQUIRIES
Info@SamuelFrench.com
1-866-598-8449

No one shall make any changes in this play(s) for the purpose of production. No part of this book may be reproduced, stored in a retrieval system, or transmitted in any form, by any means, now known or yet to be invented, including mechanical, electronic, photocopying, recording, videotaping, or otherwise, without the prior written permission of the publisher. No one shall upload this play(s), or part of this play(s), to any social media sites.

CAUTION: Professional and amateur producers are hereby warned that *AN EARLY HISTORY OF FIRE* is subject to a licensing fee. The amateur and/or professional live stage performance rights to *AN EARLY HISTORY OF FIRE* are controlled exclusively by Samuel French. Publication of this play(s) does not imply availability for performance. Both amateurs and professionals considering a production are strongly advised to apply to Samuel French before starting rehearsals, advertising, or booking a theatre. A licensing fee must be paid whether the play(s) is presented for charity or gain and whether or not admission is charged. Professional/Stock licensing fees are quoted upon application to Samuel French.

Whenever the play(s) is produced the following notice must appear on all programs, printing and advertising for the play(s): "Produced by special arrangement with Samuel French."

For all motion picture, television, and other media rights: Joyce Ketay, The Gersh Agency, 41 Madison Ave, 33rd Floor, New York, NY 10010, jketay@ gershny.com.

MUSIC USE NOTE

Licensees are solely responsible for obtaining formal written permission from copyright owners to use copyrighted music in the performance of this play and are strongly cautioned to do so. If no such permission is obtained by the licensee, then the licensee must use only original music that the licensee owns and controls. Licensees are solely responsible and liable for all music clearances and shall indemnify the copyright owners of the play(s) and their licensing agent, Samuel French, against any costs, expenses, losses and liabilities arising from the use of music by licensees.

IMPORTANT BILLING AND CREDIT REQUIREMENTS

All producers of *AN EARLY HISTORY OF FIRE must* give credit to the Author(s) of the Play(s) in all programs distributed in connection with performances of the Play(s), and in all instances in which the title of the Play(s) appears for the purposes of advertising, publicizing or otherwise exploiting the Play(s) and/or a production. The name of the Author(s) *must* appear on a separate line on which no other name appears, immediately following the title and *must* appear in size of type not less than fifty percent of the size of the title type.

AN EARLY HISTORY OF FIRE was first produced by The New Group in New York City on April 30, 2012. The performance was directed by Jo Bonney, with sets by Neil Patel, costumes by Theresa Squire, lighting by Lap Chi Chu, and sound by Ken Travis. Special thanks to Deema Aitken. The cast was as follows:

DANNY	Theo Stockman
POP	Gordon Clapp
SHIRLEY	Erin Darke
KAREN	Claire van der Boom
TERRY	Jonny Orsini
JAKE	Dennis Staroselsky
BENJI	Devin Ratray

CHARACTERS

DANNY
POP
SHIRLEY
KAREN
TERRY
JAKE
BENJI

POP *speaks with a distinct German accent. The others are all Midwestern.*

SETTING

The Mueller home in a medium-sized Midwestern town.

TIME

Early fall, 1962

For:

Jo
Theo Gordon Claire
Dennis Jonny Erin
Devin Valerie Stephanie
Sash

SCENE 1

*(The Mueller home has a claustrophobic smallness. The stage left door enters into a small kitchen with an upstage window above the sink, cabinets along the stage left wall, shelves under the sink and cabinet. A small, square, metal kitchen table. Linoleum floor. The living room has an open Castro convertible, a coffee table shoved to the side. Stage right has an upright piano with a stool against the wall. Books, photos stand atop the piano. A window above the piano feeds in light. Downstage of the piano stands a small table with a record player on top of it, a box of records under it. At the other end of the piano and under stairs that run up to a compressed second floor, a door opens into a small closet. Upstairs has two doors, one to the bathroom, the other to **POP**'s bedroom. The slant of the roof narrows and shrinks the space. A dresser stands crammed into the stage left end of the tiny hall.)*

*(Music, guitars in a swirl, and light come up on early morning. **DANNY** stands sipping a cup of coffee. He wears work clothes, matching grey trousers and shirt; work boots. He takes a quick sip of coffee, then looks up toward **POP**'s bedroom door.)*

DANNY. Pop. Hey, c'mon, can you get up? I gotta talk to you. *(He waits.)* You hear me?

POP. *(from off)* Yeah, yeah.

DANNY. *(running up, banging on the door)* Popper! C'mon. Please!

POP. *(shouting from off)* I'm up! I'm up!

*(**DANNY** knocks louder, then hurries downstairs. **POP** staggers out the door to the head of the stairs.)*

POP. *(cont.)* So damn early? We gotta talk now?

DANNY. It's important.

POP. *(starting down)* I'm sleepy, I'm tired. But you – you gotta get me up for what I don't know – Ohhhhhhhhhh! Owwwww. Owwwwwwww.

(He winces, clutching his calf, forced to sit down on the stairs.)

Cramp. Cramp.

*(**DANNY** rushes up to help, pushing **POP**'s toes back, rubbing the calf.)*

Ohhhhhh, you fix it, ohhhhhh. It's from those damn cement floors from work. *(as **POP** feels better)* Two weeks I'm off the job, I still got the hurts.

DANNY. You been gettin' a lot of these, Pop. Maybe you should get yourself checked out. Okay?

POP. *(nodding)* Okay.

*(**DANNY** lets **POP**'s foot drop, and heads back to the kitchen.)*

Now you tell me why you got me up. *(starting down)*

DANNY. You ain't awake enough yet.

POP. Whata you want me to do, jump up and down? I'm –

DANNY. – It's important – *(putting a cup of coffee on the table for **POP**)*

POP. I'm awake. See? Eyes open, arms movin'!

*(As **POP** sits at the table, **DANNY** brings a suit on a hanger from hooks by the front door.)*

DANNY. *(explaining carefully)* Karen asked me over tomorrow night for dinner, so what I want you to do is take this suit to the cleaners today and pick it up tomorrow before six.

*(As **POP** takes the suit, **DANNY** moves off to the downstairs closet.)*

I'm at work when they open and they close before I get home.

POP. *(examining the suit)* You oughta have a new suit. A good suit. You should have seen the suits I had at your age. Their quality was from another world – hand made, personally attended to by craftsman. Artists. This suit is not a suit even. What is this? Why do you want to wear such a thing?

DANNY. It's fine, Pop. *(grabbing the suit, returning it to the hook by the front door)* I look good in it.

POP. Where does she live, this Karen? *(sipping his coffee)*

DANNY. On Citadel.

POP. That's a nice neighborhood. She has a last name, this Karen?

DANNY. Edwards.

POP. And she works, where?

DANNY. She's in college – out East.

POP. Oh, oh. Maybe she can get you back to college, this wonderful, smart Karen.

DANNY. I wouldn't hold my breath on that one, Pop.

POP. What I got from my education is in my head and mine forever, and someday you will wake up to that fact. But you can't see it is all, and so you don't know what it is. Someday you will learn.

DANNY. *(bringing **POP** toast)* You gonna look for another job today?

POP. *(annoyed)* Why? Why do you say that? I will find a job.

DANNY. Yesterday's dirty dishes are still in the sink, Pop.

(**POP** *rises, starts for the stairs.*)

Where you goin'?

POP. I must change my clothes. You tell me I must go –

*(The door bursts open and **TERRY** comes in. **DANNY**'s age, smaller, dressed in mechanic's one-piece outfit.)*

TERRY. – Hi Mueller-people –

DANNY. – Terry turd –

POP. – If I am to look for a job, as you command me, must I not change my clothes –

TERRY. – We need coffee –

POP. – I'm trying to talk to you, Danny.

> (**JAKE** *comes in. He wears another kind of work outfit.*)

JAKE. Where's the coffee? I need some coffee.

> (**POP**, *grumbling, gives up on talking and goes into his room.* **JAKE** *grabs a cup, which he holds out for* **TERRY** *to fill with coffee, as he addresses* **DANNY**, *who has begun folding the Castro, returning the cushions, turning it back into a couch.*)

Hey, Dan, Janie gimme the news last night that Milly's still got the hots for you – No, kiddin'. She was sitting on the curb tearing flowers apart and sayin', "Danny loves me, he loves me not."

DANNY. I heard that.

JAKE. So after work, let's pick her up and get Janie and somebody for Terry –

TERRY. *(at the table with his coffee)* Who? Get who for Terry?

JAKE. I don't know. Who you want?

TERRY. Wanda. Let's try Wanda.

JAKE. So we get Wanda for Terry, Milly for you, and we go out to that nice spot by the river – we set the dial to where Elvis is king – let him put his sweetness out into the air. I'm gettin' a boner just thinkin' about it. Next thing you know, nobody can find their underwear. *(sitting down on the couch)*

DANNY. It's over for me and Milly. And I got somethin' else to do tonight anyway.

JAKE. Not another date with whatserface? Lulubaby? Rich bitch from on top a the hill.

DANNY. Don't call her that.

JAKE. She lives on Citadel Avenue. You got to be rollin' in dough to live up on Citadel Avenue. But I ain't prejudice. Bring her out to the river.

DANNY. We got other plans.

JAKE. Which don't have room for riffraff like us.

DANNY. Relax, Jake, because I am gonna be so good to this girl, she's gonna hand me a pile of money. And then I'm gonna buy the Blue Note Bar. Ter can be the bartender, cause he's social, and you can be the bouncer cause you like to punch people. Pop can stand around givin' it a European touch.

TERRY. That'd be great if things were like that. I mean, things are great now, but if they were like that, that'd be greater.

JAKE. It's never gonna happen.

TERRY. It could.

JAKE. But it ain't.

TERRY. I hope you get cancer.

JAKE. That's not a very nice thing to say, Terry. Milly's mom is almost dead of it.

TERRY. It ain't my fault.

JAKE. So whata we gonna do tomorrow night. Whata you wanna do?

DANNY. I can't.

JAKE. Why not? This broad again? I bet you ain't even copped a feel yet, have you.

DANNY. Terry. When's the last time you got laid? *(seated at the table to put on his work boots)*

TERRY. Why?

DANNY. Because the way Jake talks all we got to do is get Milly and Janie and Wanda out to the river and we get laid. If we're lucky, we neck and get all hot and bothered and come in our pants.

JAKE. Speak for yourself.

DANNY. Milly and Wanda are not droppin' their drawers at the drop of a hat. So let's not kid ourselves, right, Terry?

TERRY. Well, sure. Nobody wants to get nobody pregnant.

JAKE. You never heard of a rubber?

DANNY. So are you sayin' you get to screw Janie whenever you want?

JAKE. I do all right. All I know is it's gettin' so a guy needs a lousy appointment to see you. But that's okay. Because tonight's tonight and tomorrow is tomorrow and what I want is the three a us tomorrow night piggy – sloppy drunk – I mean, hammered – and rollin' around in some gutter.

DANNY. I can't, Jake. Maybe Sunday.

JAKE. Sunday? Bullshit! *(annoyed, rising, drifting to the piano)* I mean, what else you got lined up for the next year so I can fit myself in? What the hell, man?

(He flips open the cover to the piano keys.)

DANNY. Jake, what're you – no! Jake, don't!

JAKE. *(as he plinks the tune)* For old acquaintance be forgot…

DANNY. Knock it off.

JAKE. *(straightening as if stopping)* Break your crumby goddamn date!

(He slams down on the keys, a loud discordant sound.)

POP. *(from off)* Hey!

DANNY. *(crossing away)* You're on your own!

POP. *(emerging, fully dressed now, overlapping)* Hey, no playing, you know that. Go on, get away.

*(**JAKE** lowers the lid over the keys.)*

That's good. Ohhhh, that's good. Smart.

*(as **JAKE** leans against the piano)* No leaning. You don't ever touch that thing again, you hear me, *Hund!*? You do what I say –

DANNY. Popper!

POP. Why do you let him do that, Danny? Your mama is not here to protect herself. Nobody touches that.

DANNY. It's a piano. It's supposed to be touched.

POP. *(as **DANNY** moves to go out the door)* Danny, where's your lunch? You must have your lunch.

*(**DANNY** stops, wheels, and heads to the kitchen. At the top of the stairs, **POP** calls to him.)*

Where's your hat?

DANNY. I don't need a hat, Pop.

POP. You must wear a hat in this sun, or you will roast your brain. *(heading into his room)* I have one for you to borrow.

(DANNY packs a sandwich and apple into his lunch bucket.)

JAKE. I'll see ya in the car.

(JAKE starts for the door and then the door pops open, hitting him in the nose, and he yelps as BENJI enters.)

BENJI. Whoooops!

TERRY. Benji!

BENJI. You don't want to get hit by doors, don't stand in front of 'em.

JAKE. Here's a hat! *(grabbing the hat from BENJI's head)* I got a hat!

(BENJI reaches to get the hat back.)

BENJI. Hey. Thief. Hoodlum. Crook!

(JAKE tosses the hat to TERRY.)

Bunch a crooks!

(BENJI goes to TERRY who tosses the hat to DANNY.)

The story of my life. *(giving up, sitting on the couch)*

BENJI. *(cont.)* Just a bystander and all of a sudden somebody steals my hat.

(DANNY puts the hat on BENJI's head.)

DANNY. Tell Pop to be sure and take care of my suit. He's gotta pick it up by six tomorrow.

(DANNY goes out the door followed by JAKE and TERRY, who waves as POP comes out of the room, hat in hand.)

TERRY. See ya!

POP. Danny! Danny!

(But DANNY goes, shutting the door.)

BENJI. He said to tell you, Emile, he said –

POP. *(angrily coming down the stairs)* Nichts? Nothing. He says nothing but "get up, wake up, take my clothes to the cleaners" and – like that. "Do the dishes, clean the house."

(As **BENJI** *smiles at him, waves hello,* **POP** *laughs.)*

Ohhhhhhh, all my life, I have been too serious, thinking too much, thinking, thinking.

(He sits on the kitchen chair.)

A lot of years I worked, Benji. A lot of jobs. I want to sit a little is all.

BENJI. *(getting Ovaltine, milk, a glass, a spoon)* Darn tootin'. Darn tootin', Emile! You feelin' bad you quit that stupid thankless job?

POP. – No, no, I don't feel bad –

BENJI. – A man's got your brains, he don't have to take bein' told how to guard a door for crissake by some nincompoop –

POP. – I know –

BENJI. – To guard a door, you just guard it –

POP. – You guard it –

BENJI. – That's all you do. You keep a close eye on it. Clyde Brown was hollerin' at you –

POP. – that sonofabitch –

BENJI. – cause of how smart you are –

POP. – I don't want to talk about it –

BENJI. – He's a jealous man, that Brown. You can see it in how he walks. *(seated now and ready to drink his Ovaltine)*

POP. If only the chess would come. A hundred years ago we sent. What is wrong with the mail these days? And a company like that – they advertise they have this wonderful chess set, and then they tell you they have run out of it. You have to wait. They will send it when they have more. Why do they do that?

BENJI. I don't know.

POP. At the university, we played always. Our club of fine young men. And when I saw the ad in that magazine

– it was a set almost the same as the one we all loved. I said, I must have it. I will pay the price.

BENJI. Boy, oh boy, I hope I can learn. It's hard, ain't it?

POP. That's why it's a wondrous game. It brings another world. And if you had once seen Karl play, the great Karl Jaeger, my good, dear friend, you would understand. He would have become the greatest chess master of all time. But history did not care for him. Great men are often cast aside. He was Jewish and so that was that. Last night, I dreamed of him. Yes, it was last night.

BENJI. I think I had a dream about Karl Jaeger, too.

POP. Really. You did, Benji?

BENJI. I think so. The other night, and he was –

POP. My god, look at the way I am sitting.

BENJI. Huh?

POP. Look! Look!

(BENJI rises and moves to look at POP from one side and then the other.)

BENJI. What?

POP. This is the way I was sitting when Brown yelled at me and I quit. He stood where you are. That bastard Brown. Benji, you pretend to be Brown, my boss.

BENJI. Huh?

POP. You know, like when I quit and I'm sitting and he hollered at me. This is the way I was sitting. I want to show you what I did. Back up a step. *(as BENJI steps back)* Holler at me.

BENJI. What did he holler?

POP. Insults. Insults.

(BENJI sticks his hands deep into his pockets, a habit of Brown's that they both know.)

BENJI. Okay.

POP. And you must say, "You get your ass outa that chair!" And twice – you must holler twice.

BENJI. Okay.

POP. And loud!

> (**POP** *poses, sitting, then gives a signal that he is ready, and* **BENJI**, *hands in his pockets as Brown, swaggers forward.*)

BENJI. Mueller, goddammit, you dummy, get your lazy, good-for-nothing-ass-off that chair! Hey Mueller, goddammit, you –

POP. *(leaping up)* Brown, you – you – The day you walk on water, then you can be God. You want to be God, Brown, you walk on water!

BENJI. Ohhhhh! Emile, that's a good one – Is that what you said?

POP. And he stood there stupid like a dog. Boom, I slammed the door.

BENJI. That Brown is a bastard.

> *(Together, they laugh.)*

POP. A pig!

BENJI. A pig-hund!

> (*As* **POP**, *laughing, moves his dirty dishes to the sink,* **BENJI** *blurts out.*)

You know – I forgot to tell you. Boy, my head's so fulla holes, it leaks. The folks said I should start takin' these vitamins. *(Removing a bottle from his pocket, he prepares to take one.)* These are multiplied so they got everything in them.

POP. What did you forget to tell me?

BENJI. I forgot to tell you what Danny said to tell you. *(taking the vitamin, he drinks from his Ovaltine)*

POP. So do it. Tell me. What was it?

BENJI. He said – Danny said to tell you to be sure and take care of his suit and to pick it up tomorrow.

POP. Oh, his suit, his suit. It's all he can tell me. Do this, do that. Get a job. But I am not a man to shirk my duties. I will seek another job, and that will shut Danny up.

BENJI. I hear they're seekin' help over at the Murphy's filling station.

POP. Let's go. A man must work until he drops in his tracks. Is that the saying?

BENJI. One of 'em.

*(He heads for the door, with **BENJI** following.)*

POP. But first we go to the post office to see if the chess has arrived.

BENJI. Darn tootin'.

(They go.)

POP. *(offstage)* Bring Danny's suit!

*(**BENJI** hurries back, opens the door, grabbing the suit off the coat rack and shutting the door.)*

(music: guitars in a blast)

(blackout)

SCENE 2

(Music. Lights rise. The next day, about six-thirty in the evening. **DANNY**, *wearing a white shirt, a tie, socks, boxer shorts, and no pants, stands with the phone in his hand;* **TERRY** *is perched on the sink counter, looking out the window. He turns to* **DANNY**.*)*

TERRY. I don't care what anybody says, you oughta go as you are. Show off a little.

(beat)

Is it still ringing?

DANNY. Yeah, it's still ringing. I'm not just standing here.

TERRY. How many times you gonna let it ring?

DANNY. I keep thinking they might be workin' late or come back – they forgot somethin'. *(hanging up disgustedly)* I knew I shoulda done it myself. But I couldn't.

*(***DANNY*** looks at his watch, then moves to look out the kitchen window near* **TERRY**.*)*

TERRY. You know what I almost did today? On my way over I almost went up on the hill. I saw this bunch of little kids headin' up. Cowboy hats and guns. Climbin' and shoutin'. And I felt like tagging along. Things are dryin' up. It's hill burnin' season, man, that was fun – settin' them hill fires – some a the most fun we ever had.

DANNY. Right. Great. Start a fire and then work our buns off to put the stupid thing out before it spreads too far.

TERRY. *(bounding off the counter, determined to enlist* **DANNY***)* What about that time you thought you were trapped out on Indian Bluff and gonna burn alive? What about that?

DANNY. I was a kid, and there was a lot of smoke.

TERRY. You believed it though, and you really panicked till we got that log across and rescued you. One a these days, we should go up there again, you know, just walk around, see the old places, Crystal Cave and Spear Valley – see what's left. You do that with me?

DANNY. You know what'd happen? We'd hit the top a that hill with nothin' to do but stand around. So that's what we'd do – we'd stand around and then we'd come home. Unless you wanna play cowboys?

TERRY. Which we couldn't, right? *(He wheels away.)* Awwwwww, crap! You know what I wish? Sometimes I just wish I was a goddamn aborigine – a lousy stupid native in a jungle. Eat, sleep, and screw. And that's it. Everything we do is such a rotten, lousy sweat! *(facing* **DANNY***)* Do you know what I found out? My little sister tole me – if it wasn't humiliating enough, it's gotta be Janet who gives me the word. Shirley Fowler is hangin' around Fourth and Locust at all hours of the night.

DANNY. What for?

TERRY. Whata you think? Take a guess. Or do I hafta draw you a picture? I kid you not. She's got her little rear end up for sale. *(moving in to face* **DANNY** *at the kitchen table)* That's right. In this goddamn berg a' forty-eight thousand, we have got probably five at most honest-to-god prostitutes, and one of 'em is my ole girlfriend.

DANNY. For sale?

TERRY. That's right.

DANNY. For sale, Terry?

TERRY. Danny, don't make me keep saying it! I saw her – I spied, you know – she's runnin' around like the pied piper. She's divorced now, so I guess she knows the ropes and got the habit. That's my guess. Nothin' ta lose and them ta gain.

DANNY. You saw this? You saw Shirley doin' this?

TERRY. I come this close one night – if I'da said the word – we'd a been on our way to the J.P. That very minute. We both knew it. Me and Shirley. I mean, we were talkin' about it, tossin' it around. I wasn't ready to settle down. I didn't have a clue what I was gonna do – maybe get into civil service – but I didn't know.

DANNY. I thought for sure you two would end up married.

TERRY. Pretty soon we were passin' each other on the street and everything was just gone! So then before I can even start to figure it out, she marries Eddie Dolan, and then she divorces Eddie Dolan. How am I supposed to keep up?

DANNY. And then Eddie goes tearing outa town on old Route 52 and does a head-on with a tree.

(Momentarily, they are quiet, considering these strange facts.)

TERRY. I wonder how much Shirley costs.

DANNY. Terry. Would you do that? Pay for Shirley?

TERRY. Why not?

DANNY. *(rising, crossing to the refrigerator)* You want a beer?

TERRY. When I saw Karen that time you pointed her out from the car she was awful pretty, man. *(as* **DANNY** *acknowledges the fact)* Can I ask you something? Are you in love? Or is that a stupid question?

DANNY. I wish I knew. *(handing over a beer)*

TERRY. If it was me, I bet I'd be the last to know. *(pacing to sit on the couch)*

DANNY. I don't want to screw her, though.

TERRY. *(little laugh)* What?

DANNY. Not that I've had the chance. It's murder tryin' to get alone without a car. We haven't even necked much. I want to, don't get me wrong, but it feels like it's something different – it's a weird feelin' – like I might ruin somethin'. But then we're walkin' around and she bumps my arm, or we hold hands, I get a hard-on. I come home with blue balls.

TERRY. Oh boy. You're in dangerous waters, Dan.

DANNY. That day we met – she was cryin' at this bus stop. Karen was readin' this book and cryin', and when she looked up and we met eyes, I got the willies. I was so damn dirty – I'd been lugging bags of cement all day so I was like this gray monster. I didn't think she'd even talk to me.

(Fingering his tie unhappily, he leaps up and heads to the downstairs closet.)

It's like a roller coaster ride, man – I walk her up to the door and kiss her good night – she gets a look in her eyes.

(Having pulled the tie off, he tosses it into the closet, grabs another.)

All these feelings. I'm halfway afraid to get her alone. On the other hand, it's all I think about. That book she had – it's called *Catcher in the Rye*. You ever heard of it? I been readin' it.

(Using his reflection in a framed picture near the closet he ties the new tie.)

TERRY. Uh-uh. Is it good?

DANNY. I picked up a copy. And this other one she had, too.

TERRY. What are they about?

DANNY. *(breaking from the picture to face* **TERRY**) That's the thing – it's hard to know. The one is a guy, and he's not like us... Except that he is. He's tryin' to figure out his life – and he hates phonies. People doing things they don't mean and making him do things he doesn't mean. And they're everywhere, these phonies, they're coming in the windows, he says.

TERRY. So now we gotta lock the windows. Or else be overrun by phonies.

DANNY. He's right, though. I think it's true. The older I get the harder it is not to feel like everything I do is somebody else's idea. I've only read a little of the other one – it's called *On the Road* and it's about this crazy bunch and...hitchhiking. *(Pacing back to the table, he sits.)*

TERRY. You think Karen's ever been to bed with anybody?

DANNY. I don't know, but I don't think so.

TERRY. Those guys out East are slick man – that's what I hear. What are her parents like?

DANNY. Tonight's the night I meet 'em. If Pop ever gets here with that suit. Which he will. *(At the window, he looks out.)* And I will have a good time. *(moving back to the table)* I mean, just cause they got a shitload of money don't mean they ain't regular people.

*(The door opens and **JAKE** steps in, moving slowly.)*

JAKE. Listen to me. I need a shot – you got any booze. I just had a frightening experience.

DANNY. Pop's got some scotch. I'll give you one.

JAKE. Because I am suffering from – if there is such a thing – is there such a thing as Dorkaphobia? – because I am suffering from it and it's like claustrophobia except it's about dorks.

TERRY. Sure, sure, that's where there's dorks everywhere you look and you're scared you're going to end up in a small room surrounded by 'em.

DANNY. You didn't see Pop out there, did you? *(offering a shot glass of scotch)*

JAKE. No, but I did see the biggest dork in town. And who is that?

TERRY. That jerk, Bobby Jensen.

JAKE. *(downing the scotch)* Bobby Jensen! So at work this morning – on the way over – there's a snake tryin' to crawl across the road. I swerve to miss him, right? It's a clear case of he's lost. So why not give him a helping hand? So then later – on break – Jensen is braggin' about how he run the snake down. Ran over, backed over him. He's such an asshole.

DANNY. What is it about that guy? You wanna clock him.

JAKE. And yet at the same time, he's a joke – I tell him he's an asshole, and he gives me a look which is meant to scare me but I can't stop laughin'. He's actin' like his buddies better hold him back. So at lunch hour, I go up and I say, "Hey, Bobby, how 'bout you give me your autograph." *(holding up a paper bag)* I hold up my lunch bag. "Please sign it, 'King a the Snake Killers,'" I say. And I go like this.

*(He pulls the dead snake from the bag and waves it at **DANNY**.)*

DANNY. What the hell are you doing?

*(**JAKE** drops the dead, mangled snake onto the kitchen table.)*

TERRY. Is that a bull snake? *(moving warily)* That's a bull snake. Danny, you remember when we saw that bull snake eat that frog?

DANNY. *(studying the snake)* You think that's him?

TERRY. No, no.

(They all three lean in to study the dead snake on the table.)

Maybe. No, it can't be. That poor frog was scared out of his mind, and the snake was like, "Everything's copacetic."

JAKE. *(returning the snake to the bag)* I'm looking for an opportunity to bury the poor thing.

TERRY. Do you ever think about when we saw that, Danny? Sometimes out of the blue I can't stop thinkin' about the look in his eyes.

*(As **JAKE** wipes his hand on his pants, **DANNY** wipes the table top.)*

JAKE. Listen, you guys. Listen close. You gotta promise me, Danny, on Saturday, if I get Jensen down and it looks like I'm gonna kill him, somebody pull me off him!

TERRY. You mean, he wants to fight you?

JAKE. No, no, they – the whole bunch of them – want to fight us. And they want to call it a "rumble." It's all set for Saturday at one-thirty behind the ballpark.

DANNY. But how can they fight us? They're a bunch of kids – it'll be like pigmy dorks against the giant natives from the grass country!

TERRY. Jensen's a measly sophomore in high school.

JAKE. He's a junior.

DANNY. He's not even tall enough to hit you in the face!

JAKE. You can fight him on your knees.

DANNY. Wait a minute! All of a sudden I got this picture in my head of us kickin' crap outa a bunch of midgets. And it looks stupid!

JAKE. Whata you talkin' about how "it looks"! Nobody's lookin'. It's us and them and we're – What a you doin' in your goddamn underwear, anyway, tryin' to make me horny?

TERRY. He's waiting for his ole man to bring his suit so he can go to dinner at Karen's house but nobody knows where the ole guy is.

JAKE. Oh. What terrible news. What time is this dinner? *(grabbing a beer from the fridge)*

TERRY. Seven. He's gotta get goin' or he's not gonna make it.

DANNY. Terry, I can talk for myself. And I am gonna make it. *(glances at his wristwatch)* Ohh, where the hell is he? *(stepping out the door, he yells)* POPPER! COME HOME!

TERRY. *(behind* **DANNY***, yelling out the door, too)* SHANE! COME BACK, SHANE!

JAKE. *(relaxing on the couch with his beer)* Dan, I gotta give you the bad news. You ain't gonna make it. You are dead in the water.

*(***DANNY*** gives ***JAKE*** the finger and heads for the phone.)*

DANNY. I'm callin' Benji's folks. Maybe Pop is there.

JAKE. What a day I put in. They got us on piecework now, and these goddamn incentives. My incentive is to blow the place up. And before I get any supper, I gotta work for my ole man. The damn Chevy fell off the blocks, so he's worried we look like riffraff, because the chevy in our front yard is crooked.

TERRY. I'll give ya a hand.

DANNY. *(phone to his ear, begging)* Dammit, Benji, answer your phone.

JAKE. Danny, man, it's like that girl I was datin' in Chicago – she was a –

DANNY. You get that, Ter? Anybody else has a date, it's with a broad or a bitch, but he goes out and it's a "girl" and –

JAKE. Okay, this broad, this bitch, this cow, this pig, got her claws in me. Don't make no difference what we call her. The point is – to me, the point is –

DANNY. That you're still stuck on her. That's the –

JAKE. Will you let me say what I'm trying to say?

DANNY. Why the hell is she every other word outa your mouth?

JAKE. She ain't. Bullshit.

TERRY. You talk about her a lot.

*(As **DANNY** hangs up angrily and grabs his shoes. He sits at in the kitchen, fussing with the shoe.)*

JAKE. Then cause she was a good lesson. She wore that thin, flimsy, billowy stuff and she moved around, you know, shakin' and struttin' like she was so hot she could hardly stand it. But it was all just this show, and if you mistook it and dared to cop a feel, she'd give you a look like you farted in church. I mean, she had my number. I didn't even know I had a number. By the time I'd spent all my money and was about to pawn my shoes, she looks at me real sad and says, "This isn't working. We're not right for each other." So while I'm standin' there letting flies collect on my teeth, I realize she's having a ball. Tears and everything. This is the high point for her, when she gets to be this weepy nut-cruncher ditching me.

*(**JAKE** moves in on **DANNY**, who gets up and steps away.)*

DANNY. Guess what? Just because that happened to you don't mean it's gonna happen to me.

JAKE. They were assembled on the same assembly line, Linda Dotson and your rich bitch nut-cruncher.

DANNY. The truth is I don't give a damn what happened to you and this broad. I got more pressing problems.

JAKE. I'm tellin' ya. You startin' ta think maybe she's a big deal, all you're gonna get is hurt, cause she's a pretty, sweet-smellin' lie!

TERRY. He means you gotta settle up before you settle down, Dan, like you're always sayin'.

JAKE. No! That ain't what I mean. I mean, my ole lady, for example, thinks she caught my ole man with this love charm – a hunk a rope and chicken feet she got from a gypsy at a carnival, but she thinks it's why she hooked him. Danny, that's a fact! Ter! Ter, tell him that story.

(**TERRY** *has no idea what* **JAKE** *means.*)

You know, the one about your ole man up on that building with that broad and they flip the coin.

TERRY. Oh, yeah, yeah. It's just that, Dan, well – my dad and this girl – this was in Chicago and they were –

JAKE. His ole man and the broad he was goin' with at the time – see, he didn't have a job or anything, but they wanted to get married, so one night, they're up on the roof of a building and they're talkin'. Right, Ter? And so what'd they do?

TERRY. They flipped this coin. See, they decided to flip a coin – heads he'd go find a job and they'd wait – tails, they'd get married that very night. Well, Molly – her name was Molly – and Dad tole me all this one night after one too many six packs, and –

JAKE. And! Bang! They flip the stupid coin and it's heads in the palm a his hand, and so that's the end of Molly. Like she stepped off that rooftop. So Ter's old man ends up marryin' somebody else, see? You see? It's all crap, all this love crap, and you go for it, you got rocks in your head. So take my advice. Screw her and run for the hills, because –

(*The door opens.* **POP** *enters without the suit; he carries a bag of groceries. They all stare at him.*)

POP. Whatsamatter, you never saw me before?

JAKE. *(moving for the door)* Let's go, Ter. Danny. You get outa that shirt and that stupid tie. We'll be back.

POP. *(to JAKE as he and TERRY go)* Hey, you real good at giving orders. *(to DANNY)* He's always giving orders.

(POP starts unpacking groceries, putting them into the kitchen cabinet.)

DANNY. Do you know what time it is?

POP. Why? It's five minutes after seven.

DANNY. Where you been? Whata you been doin'?

POP. I played some checkers with Ralph Kress. I beat the hell out of him. *(laughing, busy with the groceries)* Danny, something I would like a lot, you and me to play chess sometime. I could teach –

DANNY. – Popper, where's it at?

POP. Huh? The chess? In the mail. The stupid –

DANNY. Goddamn, sonofabitch! *(leaping up, striding into the living room)*

POP. Ohh, no. Don't worry about it. It will come. You got to be –

DANNY. *(overlapping.)* – I'm not talkin' about your goddamn chess.

POP. What then? No, no. I don't want to know. I feel good today. I want to keep it. Why do you always want to ruin my happiness? You got nothin' to holler about anyway. I should holler. If I once could come home and supper would be on the table –

DANNY. I work all day!

POP. I worked all my life!

DANNY. You're livin' now, ain't you, but you ain't workin'.

POP. You are really something. You think you are so special. Together me and my father' – we had to kill a horse once – our good horse who broke her leg on the ice and we had to do it in the winter cold – our hands like stones and –

DANNY. You wanna go kill a horse?

POP. You shut up.

(**POP** *is about to stick the empty grocery bag under the sink.*)

DANNY. Where's the suit?

POP. What suit? What – *(He freezes, straightens.)* Ohhhhhhhh!

DANNY. You know now?

POP. Oh, Danny…I'll – *(moving for the door)* I'll go back. *(He marches for the door.)* Five minutes and the suit will be right –

DANNY. *(overlapping last words)* They're closed. The cleaners are closed.

POP. I will get them to open. Ralph Kress is neighbor to the Arnold family and he can ask –

DANNY. – No. It's too late. I'm supposed to be there now!

POP. You can telephone and say you are a little late but –

DANNY. *(overlapping last words)* Are you nuts? I'm not goin' up there late. They invited me to dinner at their house. Up on Citadel Avenue, for god's sake.

POP. You can still go. Yes, yes. Dress up without a suit. You got good shirts and pants – we can call a taxicab and – *(hurrying to the downstairs closet)*

DANNY. Without a suit it ain't right. It ain't right.

POP. But what's right? Who knows what's right? *(bringing trousers to* **DANNY** *who is on the couch)* Sometimes a good shirt and pants is even better than a suit.

(**DANNY** *takes the pants, stands, holding them in front of himself, as if to see how they might work.*)

I was going to get it. I don't know what happened. I went out to look for work because you are always complaining that you work and –

DANNY. Mr. Edwards will have a suit on. He's always in one when I pick her up. I can just see 'em up there drummin' their fingers, wonderin' where I am. *(hurling the pants away)* No! You screwed it up!

POP. Stop lookin' at me like that – like I'm disgusting, and –

DANNY. *(overlapping last words)* – But you're actin' like you had nothin' ta do with this.

POP. *(overlapping last words)* – And you cry about the tragedy of no suit. Oh, you have so much to learn.

DANNY. *(overlapping last words)* How could you not know how I wanted this to go all the way right?

POP. Your mama and I ran from a country of culture, of history being made into shit by thugs, by baboons!

DANNY. *(overlapping last words)* You forgot my suit! That's what we're talking about!

POP. It's a suit. You lost your suit.

DANNY. I didn't lose it, goddammit! You –

POP. – Nothing, nothing. You know nothing of trouble. Let them come and drag Terry off – let them drag off your friends and tell you nothing. Your mama knew. And when she died, the world ended. Again it ended.

DANNY. *(overlapping last words)* You're so full of crap. Honest to god.

POP. Do you even care about what happened to us? What am I to do with you? What will –

DANNY. You gotta stop! You gotta. *(overlapping and enraged)* I start talkin' about your screw-up and the next thing I know, it's my fault. Because you turn everything on its head, so it's my fault, or it's all the past, the goddamn past. But you forgot – because you don't give a damn – because you're playin' checkers, for god's sake!

*(**TERRY**, partway in the door, overlaps **DANNY**, shouting to get his attention.)*

TERRY. Danny, HEY! Hi, Mr. Mueller. Ya done with the speech-makin' because –

*(**POP** and **DANNY** don't move. **TERRY** has a suit on a hanger.)*

Here you go. May bag a little, but it beats goin' nude.

*(**DANNY** stares.)*

It's a suit. You know. This is a coat and these are the pants – and they match, see, so it's a suit. Like you been hollerin' for. So take it.

DANNY. I can't, no, it's all…shot…it's all –

(A car horn honks, loud, insistent.)

TERRY. Dammit, now Jake ain't gonna wait forever, let's go!

(DANNY is startled.)

You think I snuck inta Jake's house and stole his ole man's suit? It's that special one – you know, the one Jake's always braggin' his dad had it made when he went to that union convention in Atlantic City, New Jersey.

(DANNY reaches, takes the pants, pulling them on.)

Attaboy! He's riskin' life and limb – his ole man finds out, he'll kill him. Now, let's go. Jake's gonna can it and get you up there like we got a police escort. And then his brother's gonna pick us up so you can keep the car. C'mon. You can change in the car.

*(**TERRY** and **DANNY** rush for the door. **POP** stands watching. As **DANNY** hesitates, looks at **POP**. **DANNY** goes.)*

(Music. Guitars.)

(blackout)

SCENE 3

(The lights come up – night – the Mueller home. We hear **KAREN** *talking from off, and then* **KAREN** *and* **DANNY** *enter.)*

KAREN. *(offstage)* If I recall correctly, about a million times, you made an idiot out of yourself –

(They enter.)

– getting all worked up about how something almost cataclysmic would have to happen before you ever brought me to your house –

(As he turns on the lights, she holds flowers and a helium balloon on a weighted string.)

– and where am I?

*(***DANNY*** removes her jacket, ending up with the flowers. She places the weighted balloon on the table.)*

DANNY. Well, I saw your house, I thought fair's fair – let's be even-steven.

(Having taken a pitcher of ice water from the fridge, **DANNY** *pours the water into a vase.)*

KAREN. Is that ice water? You'll freeze the stems.

DANNY. You do it.

(Leaving the flowers and vase on the table, he goes to the stairs, as **KAREN** *gets water form the sink.)*

KAREN. They're living things, Danny.

*(***DANNY*** goes to check the bathroom and bedroom to see if* **POP** *is around.)*

DANNY. It didn't matter at all that I got there late, did it? I think everybody had a good time. I think they did. I was worried your father would be stuffy, you know. I was so nervous, I made myself even later, sitting out in the car trying to make up my mind whether to come in or not. *(heading back down)*

KAREN. That was the one really hard part – when you were already late and then we saw you sitting out in the car for another five minutes.

DANNY. You saw me? You all saw me? What about when I came in, did they notice the suit was big? That's why I was late. I mean, there was this whole magilla about my suit. I mean, when you were in the kitchen with your mother, doin' secret lady things, did she knock my suit?

KAREN. Why would she do that?

(**DANNY** *hurries into the living room, to turn on the light, she follows with the flowers.*)

DANNY. Well, it's not mine, so it's not my size.

KAREN. I don't think anybody even noticed.

(*With the flowers on the coffee table, she sits on the couch.*)

DANNY. Well, they could have. And your father in that sport coat – I damn near had a conniption when I saw him in a turtle neck, I'd been so worried he'd be stuffy. Then I have a tie on and he doesn't.

KAREN. You were being very mean to these flowers, weren't you. It's one of the eternal mysteries, the pleasure boys derive from being mean. (*Making a claw with her hand, she paws at him.*) Hisssssss!

DANNY. Ohh, great. Animal imitations.

KAREN. Cats and dogs. Boys and girls.

(*She goes to the piano and places the flowers on top, where eight or ten books stand between bookends.*)

DANNY. And snakes. Jake brought a dead snake in here today.

KAREN. (*taking out and examining several books*) Into the house? Why would he do that?

DANNY. Well, Jake, I mean – I don't know exactly.

KAREN. I must meet this guy – he sounds really awful. (*eyeing the piano*) Who plays the piano?

DANNY. Nobody.

KAREN. You just have it standing here?

DANNY. We need it for balance. The floor's warped, see, there's a few problems in the foundation so its out of kilter, and if the piano wasn't there, the whole building'd just flip.

KAREN. How incredibly exciting. You're living in a house that could capsize.

DANNY. *(On the couch, he pulls the sleeves of his jacket down over his hands.)* Ain't this the neatest suit? I borrowed it off this giant. They hadda notice. Tell the truth. What'd your mom really say about the suit when you were off in the kitchen talking.

KAREN. Danny, we didn't talk about your suit. *(joining him on the couch)* We were slaving in the kitchen, making dinner, which you didn't exactly lavish compliments on.

DANNY. I said it was good. Didn't you hear me?

KAREN. "Good." Mother slaves for hours and you say, it's "good."

DANNY. *(nervously, digging out a cigarette)* I don't know how to say that kind of stuff. It was good so I said, "Good." I didn't want to sound phony.

KAREN. *(reaching for him to give her a cigarette)* Lemme have one too.

DANNY. Just don't, okay?

KAREN. But I want to.

DANNY. You don't have to act so tough with me – you really don't.

KAREN. I smoked ciggie-boos by the bushel back East. *(heading for her purse on one of the hooks by the front door)* We just left the house so quickly I didn't have a chance to grab my pack.

DANNY. It don't look right, you know?

KAREN. What?

DANNY. A girl who looks like you smoking.

KAREN. I don't care what I look like. I'm having a nicotine fit. *(She starts rooting in her purse.)* I do have something, though, that I brought back from school for a special occasion.

*(She finds what she's looking for and, with her back to **DANNY**, tucks it into her bra, then returns to the couch.)*

I was just so nervous the way things started you're lucky you didn't walk in and find me plastered. My father's scarfing down his third martini and my date is out in his car doing mysterious things, a girl needs a lift.

(As she reaches for his lit cigarette, he pulls it out of her reach.)

DANNY. So they're mad I'm late, and watching me out the window, and then I come in, lookin' like a clown in this stupid suit.

KAREN. Danny, don' worry about it. Please can I have a cigarette? Just one puff. Please. Then we can move on to a more scintillating topic of conversation.

*(Now he surrenders the cigarette and **KAREN**, positioning herself elegantly, takes a puff and exhales.)*

Now what's wrong with how I look? *(rising, walking in the same elegant manner)* I would imagine I look quite sophisticated. Don't I?

(Running her hand along the row of books on top of the piano, she takes one and opens it.)

Are you aware that the overwhelming majority of your books pertain to sailboats. And this one has the rather emphatic inscription: "This book belongs to Danny Mueller," and then your address.

DANNY. It was just this stupid hobby from when I was little. It was a daydream – a lot of hot air. But we actually thought we were going to sail down the river. We even trained to be able to do it.

KAREN. My brother, Bryan, had a yen to travel.

DANNY. Oh, yeah? Did he do it?

KAREN. Oh, yes. Indeed he did. In every possible way. He was a winged boy.

DANNY. Where's he live now?

KAREN. *(She picks up another book.)* Holy moly. Here's one on scuba diving. Scuba diving! Did you want to do that, too?

DANNY. I thought I did. Where's your brother now? Is he at home?

KAREN. Did you see him?

DANNY. No.

KAREN. *(picking a small framed photo off the piano)* Who's this?

DANNY. Pop.

KAREN. This is your father? What a cute little tyke he was.

DANNY. Where did Bryan end up?

KAREN. *(She sets the photo down on the coffee table.)* Hey, you didn't tell me who plays the piano.

DANNY. You want something to drink? *(moving to the kitchen)*

KAREN. Are you trying to get out of telling me who plays the piano? *(Backing up, she leans against the piano.)* I'm not budging. I'm paralyzed. Do you play? Is it another one of your secret, unexpected –

DANNY. No.

KAREN. So who does? Remember. I'm not budging.

DANNY. Oh. I see. Okay. Have a ball. *(going to the refrigerator for a beer)* Why are you making such a big deal out of this? You want a Pepsi?

(She stays at the piano, leaning, silent, teasing.)

I don't wanna talk about it. What's wrong with that?

(But she won't relent, and with his beer, he studies her.)

DANNY. *(cont.)* So okay…

…you'll stand there and sooner or later starve and your skin'll get all shriveled and you'll wilt. Until you end up like…the little old piano player, lunch maker, dish washer.

KAREN. Ahhh. Lunch maker. Dish washer. Sounds like female traits. Could it be your mother?

DANNY. You got it.

KAREN. So what does she like to play? Is it pop tunes or classics? Does she have a favorite composer? *(moving toward him, happy in victory)*

DANNY. Actually, she's dead.

KAREN. Your mom is dead? Oh, Danny, I'm sorry. What happened to her?

DANNY. Well what happened is Pop and I killed her. We worked her to death.

KAREN. What?

DANNY. Sorry you asked?

KAREN. No. I mean, I'm not sorry I asked. I'm sorry I upset you, but…

DANNY. I'm not upset.

(But he is, his mood darkened; after a beat she tries to brighten the moment.)

KAREN. On the picnic tomorrow, do you know what we could do? Not scuba dive exactly, but the lake is spring fed and so very clear. We could buy some diving masks and snorkels, and then we could explore the lake.

DANNY. I been meaning to tell you I can't go on the picnic tomorrow.

KAREN. But you said you would go, Danny. When Daddy asked you, you said, "Great. You'd love to."

DANNY. *(annoyed)* I mean, your father's putting all this pressure on me. He's smiling and inviting me, and it's this big deal for him – what am I supposed to do, say, "No"?

KAREN. If you don't want to go – yes.

DANNY. I didn't want to seem rude.

KAREN. Now I'm going to be stuck out there with my parents all alone. What's so important that you can't cancel?

DANNY. It's Jake and Ter and me, and they're counting on me.

KAREN. For what?

DANNY. *(resentful, a kind of bragging)* We been friends all my life, and I gave 'em my word. We met in the first grade and we been friends ever since. Little kids up on the hill, playing cowboy. Starting hill fires. Until we had shotguns and twenty-twos. And then we went hunting. If you want to call it that. Rabbits, birds, squirrels. We shot everything we could see.

KAREN. Okay. But what does any of that have to do with tomorrow?

DANNY. There's something I hafta do with them – we hafta have this fight. It's maybe hard for you to get, because girls don't have friends the way guys do. But I hafta be there.

KAREN. Are they mad at you? If they're such friends of yours, why are you fighting them? Fight them some other day.

DANNY. Not them. It's these other guys. Not that it's going to be a real fight – we'll just push these dorks around a little – but there's a lot of them, a whole herd, but they're little and –

*(As **DANNY** sits on the arm of the couch, **KAREN**, annoyed, paces into the kitchen, where she fiddles with the balloon, poking it, grabbing the string.)*

KAREN. I'm having some trouble here, because it sounds like you're saying you'd rather be out somewhere pushing dorks than spending the afternoon with me.

DANNY. It's a kind of loyalty thing.

KAREN. What's loyal about having this not-real fight with dorks? *(coming toward him with the balloon)*

DANNY. It's Jake and Ter, see. So I gotta. The truth is, I don't even want to go, but –

KAREN. Then don't.

DANNY. I hafta! I tole you.

KAREN. *(batting the balloon so it hits him)* Bye balloony bye!

DANNY. Don't get mad. Are you mad?

KAREN. It's a game! *(batting the balloon at him)* Like everything else. You hit it back, hit it. Bye balloony BYE!

DANNY. *(He hits it.)* Bye! I just can't get out of it, okay?

KAREN. Bye! *(hitting the balloon)* No –

(DANNY pops the balloon with his cigarette. She lunges into him with both hands, shoving him back onto the couch.)

You lose. The winner of the balloony bye thing contest gets a prize.

(He flashes with anger, and as he is standing up, KAREN leans in and kisses him. Then backs away. He moves to her, kisses her, and she pulls back.)

Now…now…close your eyes…close them. *(brushing a hand over his eyes)* Let me surprise you.

DANNY. What…?

KAREN. Shhhhhhhhhh. *(her hand over his eyes, then backing away)* No peeking, Danny. One second. *(bringing out a joint from her bra)*

DANNY. What? What are you doing?

(He looks and finds her at the coffee table, where she has picked up his lighter. With the joint in her mouth, she is ready to light up.)

KAREN. Candy's dandy and liquor's quicker, according to Ogden Nash. But pot is best of all, according to the girls at school. *(as she lights and inhales)*

DANNY. You don't have any pot. You mean marijuana? That's not marijuana.

KAREN. Then try it and see. *(offering it to him)*

DANNY. Where'd you get it?

(As he reaches to take the joint, she spins away.)

KAREN. We could have so much fun tomorrow at the lake, Danny. I have a two-piece bathing suit I want to wear for you. It's bright scarlet like the letter. I love grass.

(At the record player she searches the records.)

We could go off together – there's a cabin off from the main house. Wouldn't you like that? First we could explore the underwater world, and then…

(As she has put on a record, the music starts. She moves to the music.)

Let's dance. *(kicking off her shoes, she dances toward him, around him)* What floor is this, fella? Is this the dancing floor? There's only two you know. One's for dancing, the other's for screwing. *(swirling off)*

DANNY. What?

KAREN. You heard me.

(Spinning, her back to him. **DANNY** *moves in on her, taking hold of her.)*

What? What, Danny – what are you doing?

DANNY. You know what.

KAREN. Danny, no.

(He backs her to the table, onto the table, kissing her.)

(lying on the table) Oh, Danny, Danny. Ohhhh, ohhhh.. Nooo. *(as he kisses her throat, gropes her breasts)* Don't. No. Please. Ohhhhhhhh. Noo, noo.

*(***DANNY*** suddenly stops, startled. He straightens, knowing he's wrong, he backs away.)*

DANNY. Sorry.

KAREN. *(still flat on the table, in a haze of confusion)* Wait, what? *(sitting up)* Why did you stop?

DANNY. What? I mean, you said – Oh, man – What? *(racing to the record player)* Ahhhhhhhhh. What am I doin'? *(turning off the music)* I mean, it don't matter to me what happened out East with those slick, sleazy bastards. It don't, and maybe you think it's the only thing I want from you, but it's not. There's something else – I don't know what, but you're just the most beautiful thing I ever saw. But I could hurt you. *(close to her, hoping to* *apologize)* I don't want to, but sometimes I'm a jerk in a lot of ways I don't mean to be.

KAREN. Oh, I'm having a really scary thought.

DANNY. *(backing away)* No. You don't have to be afraid.

KAREN. *(seated on the table)* Oh, but I do. It's a very, very scary thought. You know at that bus stop where we met. You know – the bus stop and everything. It's like *Lady Chatterley's Lover.*

DANNY. What is?

KAREN. Us. Us. It's a book, a novel, and it was a big mistake I think that I read it. Lady Chatterley is this very complex woman who takes up with this man, this caretaker on her estate. They have a love affair. And he's like this earth force. I mean, there you were at the bus stop with this battered old lunch bucket under your arm. Dirt on your face. Just caked into your clothes. You see how I could make the mistake. Somebody simple, I thought. Salt of the earth. Very unlike myself. Unlike my brother. A rock, you know.

DANNY. What's the scary thought?

KAREN. Well, you're deep, aren't you. You're very deep. Not a rock. Not an earth force.

DANNY. What's the matter?

KAREN. I mean, it's uncanny. God! How does this happen? *(getting off the table, desperate to understand, to explain)* It's like we have like radar and it's set to the frequency of what we think we need the least, what we think we're running from, but it finds it, this radar, and it takes us to it and we're embracing it before we even know it. I think I should go. I better go. Where's my coat?

(She scurries to find her coat, her shoes, as he tries to stay with her, to soothe her.)

DANNY. What? No.

KAREN. My brother is insane, did you know that?

DANNY. It's okay. C'mon.

KAREN. Did you know that?

DANNY. No. You said he traveled.

KAREN. *(putting on her shoes)* Well I was speaking metaphorically as opposed to – factually. His name is Bryan.

DANNY. You told me.

(He tries to hold her, but she will not have it, breaking free, putting on her jacket, grabbing her purse.)

KAREN. I mean it. I really mean it. Will you take me home? I'll walk if I have to, but –

DANNY. No. No. You don't have to walk. I'll take you. I'm sorry. I screwed it all up.

*(The door opens and **POP** enters, carrying a book. Startled for a second, he then understands.)*

POP. Oh. Hello. Hello. You're Karen, of course. *(stepping forward to shake hands)* I'm Danny's father

KAREN. I'm Karen Edwards. I'm so pleased to meet you.

POP. How do you do?

KAREN. Very well, thank you.

POP. What's that smell? Something sweet.

KAREN. I bet it's the flowers. We brought some flowers. What are you reading? May I ask? Is it a book on boats like – ?

POP. Oh, no. Chess! Danny is the boats. This is chess.

KAREN. My brother loves chess.

POP. You hear that, Danny? He won't play. He does not like anything unless it's dumb. I don't know why. Maybe you can get him to explain it to you. *(starting up the stairs)* I come to get my diploma, that's all. Some of the men at the tavern didn't believe I got one, and then Benji says, "Go get it, Emile. Show 'em."

DANNY. You don't want to keep them waiting.

POP. Danny, don't worry, I'll be on my way – I'll be getting out of your hair.

*(**POP** goes into the bedroom, with **DANNY** watching closely, as if bursting with an idea, and as the door closes, he moves toward **KAREN**.)*

DANNY. You know what I'm thinking – it's crazy, and I know it, but let's do it – stay up all night and then get downtown first thing in the morning and get a license and find a JP and fix it so we can be happy ever after.

KAREN. What?

DANNY. Let's do it.

KAREN. Are you saying you want to get married?

DANNY. Don't you?

KAREN. Did you just propose?

DANNY. Are you saying you don't want to get married – that's not what you want?

KAREN. I don't think so.

DANNY. But why would I do that then, unless it's what you wanted and somehow I knew it? *(Deflated, retreating, he sits down on the couch.)* Because it's not what I want.

KAREN. Want to see something cute?

(He looks over and she lifts her skirt and slip high, flashing him, holding them up.)

DANNY. What the hell are you doing? *(looking up, fearful of* **POP** *coming out)*

KAREN. I don't know.

DANNY. Put your dress down. What are you doing?

KAREN. I said I didn't know.

(He hurries to her and pulls the skirt down. And she flees to the corner of the couch, where she huddles, a ball of embarrassment.)

I have to escape. *(huddled, hoping to explain both his actions and her own)* I think it must be the era, you know – this particular instant in our conversation. The epoch. The fifties are hanging onto us and they're warped. They won't let go. That's what I think. It's 1962 and everything is still inside out. There's a better time coming. The fifties are a nightmare from which we have to, we have to WAKE UP.

POP. *(calling from off)* Danny! Danny!

(He comes out of the bedroom and down the stairs.)

Guess who come strutting into the bar like everybody there was just waiting for him to show up. Brown. Brown is a bully where I used to work, Karen. Off work he thinks he's still the boss. *(eager to impress her, the story is for her)* "Hi, men," he says. Everybody says, "Hello, hello." But I am on my feet, I got my nose right in his face. "You sonofa – " I'm sorry, but I curse him. I tell him, "You don't come to a table where I am sitting." He laughs, nervously. "Whatsamatter, Emile, you still mad?" "No, I'm not mad. Getting out from under you is the best thing that ever happened to me, you – " Again I curse him! *(he shrugs to* **KAREN***)* I say what I think. You live under the Nazis, you're waiting every day because you know you've said things – But I must go. The men are waiting.

(About to go, he notices the photo of himself as a child on the coffee table.)

You have my photo here? Why?

KAREN. I'm sorry. I wondered who it was.

POP. *(moving in to examine the photo with her)* Little Emile Mueller before his life was lived. How sweet. How sad. I look off.

KAREN. You have such a sweetness in your eyes. Doesn't he, Danny?

DANNY. *(pacing off to sit at the kitchen table)* Yeah.

POP. But what am I seeing and does it cause the look in my eyes?

(The door opens and **BENJI** *rushes in.)*

BENJI. Emile, what happened? They're getting drunker and talkin' stupider. Richter is sayin' you don't have a diploma.

(as **POP** *waves the diploma)* I tole 'em I saw it.

POP. Yes, Benji. I am with you.

(They go for the door.)

BENJI. I'm gonna give that damn Richter a good one square in the nose, he don't shut up.

(**BENJI** *hurries off, but* **POP** *lingers by the door.*)

POP. Karen, you must let me ask you. Your name. Edwards. That is English. But your mother, I wonder – I have a curiosity – if I would not seem rude – her family name was…?

KAREN. Hueber.

POP. German. You see. It is as I thought. Your countenance gave you to me. (*Going to the door, he turns back and smiles.*) Lebe wohl, meine Liebe, Karen. Live well, my love, Karen. *Auf Wiedersehen.*

(*And* **POP** *goes, closing the door.* **KAREN** *stands, looking at the door, then at* **DANNY**, *who sits at the table facing out.*)

DANNY. I'm gonna have a drink. I'm gonna have a very large drink and I'm gonna gulp it.

KAREN. Me, too, okay?

DANNY. We've been driven to drink.

(*He darts over to the kitchen shelves for the bottle of scotch.*)

KAREN. I need a jolt. Everything's still much too defined, much too differentiated. (*Taking off her jacket, she goes to the couch.*) Still singular and literal and so… incomprehensible.

(**DANNY** *arrives at the couch with the bottle, two glasses. He pours and she throws back a shot.*)

(*Wincing with the effect, she holds out her glass for more.*)

Swift and devastating.

(*She throws down another, and winces again.*)

Eggggggg. Does drinking this stuff ever get any easier? I think we need some transubstantiation.

(*She shoves out the glass and* **DANNY** *pours another.*)

KAREN. *(cont.)* My father, the mellow charmer you met tonight – do not believe one word of it. He called me once from Center City – he was out on business, he said he was lonely so I met him and we had chicken Kiev and rack of lamb. And then he got around to what he really wanted and he kept at it until I agreed to lie and say that my brother was not insane, but rather had run away to enlist in the Peace Corps. I had to help my father, he was so…pathetic. And my brother is a… well, what is he? A phantasm. And me? I am – not exactly a liar but I am an in-acc-u-ra-cist. I indulge in inaccuracies. Because none of any of what I just said is precise enough or sufficiently…I was twelve and Bryan went west. Came back to sit and talk in the cemetery. He liked the gravestones. He said they were a fallen empire. I'd feel nearly dizzy sometimes. He was so brilliant. He wove…circles around me…and I'm a 152 I.Q. That means I know my arithmetic. And once, leaping eagerly into what he thought was a current of enriching thought, whoosh! he disappeared, headlong into the dark…from whose…mystery…we are still awaiting his return.

DANNY. Where is he now?

KAREN. Bryan? Well, locked away at the Carney Institute in Madison, Wisconsin, since April 12th, 1960. I wanted to help him, you know – I couldn't understand – and then I ran into Salinger.

DANNY. Who's this now?

KAREN. Sorry, sorry, sorry. J.D. Salinger. He wrote that book I was reading at the bus stop.

DANNY. Oh, yeah. I picked that up.

KAREN. *(surprised)* You did?

DANNY. And the other one, too. *(shyly sliding down to sit on the floor with the bottle)* I been readin' *Catcher in the Rye*.

KAREN. Have you? *(interested)* Well, brothers – mysterious brothers are common in his work…with madness reoccurring…but as an almost saintly benediction. With Holden and Phoebe in *Catcher* it seemed he was writing about my life – about me and my brother – it really did. My brother was young and troubled. Okay. Mad. I believed – I still believe that he could help me save my brother. He had to be a seer, this Salinger. I was desperate, awaiting his somewhat irregular fictional output like someone awaiting divine instructions.

(beat)

Not that I was alone – we were a widespread following, the adolescent and fanatical. Did we all have a mad brother? He would have loathed our devotion, the ego of it, and we knew it, and yet we hoped he would continue his effort on our behalf. But then a missive came that left us confounded.

(reverential) Franny and Zooey. By now I was actually attending college in the East, just like Franny. It seemed – we feared that it was possible he had made his definitive statement.

(Her need to understand intensifies.)

And what was it? Nobody knew. Franny was in the midst of a breakdown. And Zooey was offering – if he was offering anything – this advice that none of us could grasp. My entire dorm was full of dismay, floor upon floor of little cubicles with weeping girls because we were all Franny somewhere in our souls. Perplexed girls, our brows knitted, sat with our paperback editions all over the campus grass – under trees, against stone walls. We argued and wept over the meagre pages with their incomprehensible declaration because we were being told that everybody was the fat lady who Seymour, the mad brother, had said was God – that everybody was the fat lady who was Christ. *(fearful that she may never understand)* And the only tool we were given to approach this incomprehensible instruction – the single tool to assimilate this totally incomprehensible declaration – was to say the name of God, over and over – to do like Franny and say the Jesus Prayer.

(beat)

KAREN. *(cont.)* So there we were at that bus stop, and you saw me and I saw you and we liked our looks. But you're just like Bryan.

I'm looking to latch onto a strong back and a weak mind, somebody to simplify my overly complicated goddamn thought processes, to eliminate them, so to speak, so I don't have to think, and I pick you, and all the reasons I'm thinking of aren't the real reasons. The real reasons are sailboats and underwater devices. Because you're drowning. Boys, boys! I don't get it. *(leaning down to touch* **DANNY***)* Danny, what do you want? And don't say you don't know, because you're thinking about it all the time.

DANNY. I wanna go somewhere.

KAREN. Where?

DANNY. I don't know. There's this feeling –

KAREN. What feeling?

DANNY. It's hard to explain.

KAREN. That's okay.

DANNY. It's a way I'd like to feel. I'd like to find some way to feel it.

KAREN. Are you going to look for it?

DANNY. I don't know where to look or if I have the guts.

KAREN. Have you ever had this feeling?

DANNY. I sort of had it.

KAREN. Where?

DANNY. It was dumb. It might sound dumb.

KAREN. Where was it?

DANNY. Kicking a football.

KAREN. Kicking a football?

DANNY. Yeah.

KAREN. Oh. Kicking a football. In a game.

DANNY. In practice, too. I still got the shoes. You want to see the shoes? *(moving to the downstairs closet)*

KAREN. Yes.

DANNY. I felt clean. You know? *(Leaning into the closet, he takes out the shoes.)*

KAREN. You kick it in practice, even with these shoes…and you feel clean. So go do it. You should go do it. Don't you have a football? I can buy you one. I'd love to buy you one.

DANNY. *(Returning behind the couch, he hands her the shoes.)* See, the hard square toe is where you hit it. And it wasn't just the kicking, but putting it through the goalpost. When I played, I did that, too, and –

KAREN. And you got this feeling?

DANNY. I did.

KAREN. So you need one of those, too, one of those fence things they kick it at.

DANNY. Goalposts. You kick it through.

KAREN. Let's get one of those, too. We can do it.

DANNY. But it doesn't work anymore. I can't go around kicking footballs the rest of my life. *(returning to sit on the couch)*

KAREN. Why?

DANNY. You're making fun of me, aren't you?

KAREN. No.

DANNY. How can I do that? Be realistic, okay?

KAREN. What are you talking about then? I misunderstood. I'm sorry I misunderstood.

DANNY. What I want is something else, I don't know what it is but I know the feeling. I would spend hours sometimes – kicking and kicking, over and over.

KAREN. So okay, if I understand you, what you want to do is find something that will give you the feeling you got from kicking a football.

DANNY. I tole you it would sound stupid.

KAREN. I'm not saying that. You said it made you feel clean. What made you feel dirty?

DANNY. That's a good question. But I don't know the answer. In high school I kicked points after, you know, and I kicked off, but nobody even tried field goals much. And then I got a chance. It was late in the game and it was raining and everybody on both sides had the Asian flu so nobody scored a touchdown and it was still nothing to nothing with maybe a minute to go and we were down on their twenty and coach said to kick a field goal. It was one a those from the second my foot hit it, it was perfect – all the way through me, this jolt, this kind of electrical jolt, and I knew it was going to be good. Until I looked up. And there was this guy from the other team, this big tall guy comin' up into the air – his arms up to knock it back at me

KAREN. Ohhhhhhhhhhh. Why'd he do that? Is that fair?

DANNY. I'm gonna take you home. *(But he doesn't rise.)*

KAREN. What?

DANNY. *(sinking from the couch to the floor where he sits)* I think I should.

KAREN. Nooo. *(as he shudders and bows his head in his hands)* What's a matter? Danny. Whatsamatter?

DANNY. I don' know. *(beginning to weep)* I keep missing. I just keep missing. That's what I feel. I listen when I should be talking, when I should be angry... I'm smiling. Whatever I do, it keeps making me miss what I should be doing.

KAREN. Shhhhhhhh. Shhhhhhhhh.

(As she touches him, he recoils.)

DANNY. First I'm late and then I sit out there in the car like this asshole. What an asshole! Because a this suit. I got a sweetheart of a suit – not a goddamn pink turtle neck like your ole man... *(his unhappiness turning into rage)* ...but a fine lookin' suit that fits and I spent good money for and it got left at the cleaners – I wouldn't buy a stupid suit that fits like this piece of shit in a million years. *(rising up, ripping the coat off, flinging it down)*

KAREN. Danny, nobody cared.

DANNY. They did. I know they did. I felt 'em laughin' at me, but I just couldn't admit it.

KAREN. Nooooo. Noooooo.

DANNY. *(pacing off from her)* The truth is, the whole thing was so lousy rotten I thought I was gonna throw up. I wanted to bust your ole man toothless! I mean, what are you? What is it you got, or you think you got? Everybody I ever met who had a little money, actin' all the time like they got somethin' nobody else in the world knows what it is – and it's not just the money, and not just the clothes – it's this actual belief that they are better because – BECAUSE of the money and the clothes. Makin' me so goddamn nervous, because I believe them. I believe them. *(Glaring at her, he points at the kitchen chair behind her.)* Get up on the chair. Get up on it and stand there.

KAREN. What?

DANNY. Go on. *(rushing to her, dangerously angry)* GO ON!

(And she scurries out of her shoes and up onto the chair. She stands there and he backs away a step, looking at her.)

Where is it? What is it? *(looking, needing to see)* I don't see it. I don't see it! *(He wheels away and flops onto the floor.)* I don't see a thing.

(For a moment she gazes down at him.)

KAREN. Oh, you're stony, baby. You don't even know what a lonely orbit you're in. You're Sputnik, way out there, this very private satellite, launched to where the air is thin. I'm the extraterrestrial. *(stepping down)* I'm the heavenly body.

(She advances, strides over the arm of the couch and onto the couch.)

One spooky bitch. You're the creature from the black lagoon and I'm the dark lady of the sonnets come down to screw you big time…eliminate your goddamn thought process… *(She settles onto him.)* …turn you into a prince.

(Outside there are distant sirens. A faint redness stains the sky, as she kisses him. There are sirens, growing closer, louder. **DANNY** *holds her, kissing her passionately. And then he kisses her neck, burrows in her breasts.)*

Danny, Danny – you, you…

(He leaps up and hurries to the door.)

Where are you going?

DANNY. I should lock the door.

KAREN. *(falling back onto the couch)* I know, sweet baby…love. You just don't know…all the crazy little dreams. Oh, listen to the sirens.

*(***DANNY**, *having locked the door, is trying to open a prophylactic as he hurries back.)*

You don't need that. No. I'm on the pill.

DANNY. What?

(He is with her on the couch as she tries to take the prophylactic from him and he tries to open it.)

KAREN. You don't need that thing. You really don't. We can do it to the sirens. They can be our siren…song.

(She finally gets it away and slaps it down on the coffee table.)

DANNY. What pill?

KAREN. The pill. It's a pill that won't let me get pregnant.

DANNY. You're kiddin' me.

KAREN. No. I kid you not.

(As the sirens pass by outside, they kiss and move forward to make love. The door rattles. And then there is knocking.)

TERRY. *(offstage)* DANNY! DANNY! YOU IN THERE?

*(***DANNY** *doesn't answer; they kiss and fondle and there is more pounding.)*

DANNY. GO AWAY!

TERRY. DANNY, MAN, INDIAN BLUFF IS BURNING. *(pounding hysterically)*

DANNY. TERRY, GO AWAY!

TERRY. *(shouting, pounding)* But we need the car. You got the keys.

>*(**DANNY** and **KAREN** continue to kiss on the couch, but **TERRY** will not relent, having a tantrum of cries and pounding.)*

>Danny! Danny! DANNY!!

DANNY. Oh, for god's sake.

>*(**DANNY** scurries to open the door and hand **TERRY** the car keys. As he turns away, **TERRY** grabs him.)*

TERRY. Don't you wanna come with us?

DANNY. No, I don't. *(pushing **TERRY** to go)*

TERRY. What?! Danny, what are you talking about?

>*(**TERRY** grabs **DANNY**, pulling at him, and then **JAKE** steps in.)*

JAKE. You guys are takin' forever. C'mon!

>*(**POP** and **BENJI** are heard approaching.)*

>*(**BENJI** and **POP** rush in.)*

POP. Big, fire, big – ohhhhhhh –

BENJI. I got my folks' car – we can go –

>*(**DANNY** is with **JAKE**, trying to explain what was going on with **KAREN**, that he wants to be alone.)*

POP. We can go in Benji's car! The four of us together.

TERRY. We're goin', too. You wanna go with us or them?

JAKE. You know you wanna come with us.

POP. *(taking **KAREN** by the hand, lifting her)* Karen, you don't want to miss it!

BENJI. C'mon! *(hurrying to the fridge)*

POP. So big – it's down almost to Prescott Street, Karen.

Come, come.

(**POP** *brings* **KAREN** *toward the door, and close to* **DANNY**, *as she grabs her shoes, her jacket, her purse.*)

JAKE. You guys can follow us!

TERRY. It's spreading to Spear Valley!

POP. You wait, Karen. You will see.

(**POP** *has* **KAREN**'s *hand, and in the hubbub,* **DANNY** *is reaching for* **KAREN** *who reaches for him as* **BENJI** *comes between them and* **POP** *moves her toward the door.*)

BENJI. Never a fire so big before.

(*Suddenly they are all gone,* **DANNY** *facing the open door. He trudges to the couch, grabs his coat, and trudges out the door as the sirens grow louder, the fire more intense.*)

(*blackout*)

ACT II
SCENE 1

(The scene is again the Mueller home. It is late the same night, the hours moving into morning.)

*(Music, and then a lighter flares and lights a cigarette. **TERRY**, **JAKE**, and **SHIRLEY** are in the kitchen. **TERRY** is standing at the window, his back turned to the table. He is looking out at the hill, which is still faintly glowing. **SHIRLEY** is seated at the table and **JAKE** is standing opposite her. He has one foot up on a chair and is leaning toward her, explaining something very important.)*

JAKE. Dan and me. Blood and bone. All we are. But he's got somethin' I don't have and I'll admit it – it's like this fuel additive. Terry's seen it.

TERRY. I couldn't count how many times I seen him beat his fists bloody on some wall.

JAKE. That's him tryin' to keep from killin' somebody. So he hits a wall. You know what I mean, Shirl?

SHIRLEY. He's just Danny. He's always been that way. Somethin' happens to him.

JAKE. I can't put my finger on it. You're in a bar – some wise ass is makin' remarks, and Danny don't wanna fight, he don't. So the guy thinks Danny's chicken, and then the guy says Danny's chicken. Danny still don't wanna fight. Next thing I know somethin' else happens – I never quite see it, I can be lookin' right at him, but it makes Danny nuts. You shoulda seen him, Shirl, comin' through this bunch a guys this one time – head down, knees pumpin', like he's runnin' in football. He scared me, man – he looked like one of those rabid raccoons who are foaming at the mouth. Everything's a blur – it's all arms and legs and a lot of noise. All of a sudden we broke free. We're runnin' down the street to Maury's to get us some beer. Next thing we know, there's a couple of girls who wanna go out in the car and neck. And it was their idea. Pretty neat.

SHIRLEY. Whatcha doin', Terry? You got the yimmey-yammeys?

TERRY. Indian Bluff up there looks like coal in a furnace. We don't know where Dan is but we're in his house. I think we should go.

JAKE. No, man, we're gonna stay and find out how he made out among the upper crust the second he shows. Get a detailed report.

TERRY. I do have the yimmey-yammeys and they're getting worse. What if his dad shows up first? Jake, let's arm wrestle. *(moving to the table, and they grab hands)* Shirley, you can cheerlead.

JAKE. So all of a sudden you're Charles Atlas.

SHIRLEY. *(as the boys struggle)* Rah! Rah! Boom! Boom!

TERRY. Dynamic Tension and bowls of Wheaties.

SHIRLEY. Ter, goooo! Rah, Rah! Boom, boom!

JAKE. You ain't foolin' around.

*(They struggle and grunt, **JAKE** forcing **TERRY**'s arm down with a thump. Both boys jump up.)*

SHIRLEY. I thought you had him, Terry.

JAKE. *(pacing toward the stairs, carrying the scotch bottle)* You know what I wish? Sometimes I pray for it. Another shot at those punks messed me over in Chicago and my friends are with me. It bugs me, man. I mean, the fact that those jerks are out there walkin' around somewhere in this world right now, thinkin' they took care a me – which they did – but I was dumb.

TERRY. You shouldn't dwell on it, Jake.

JAKE. I ain't dwelling on it. Get me a beer.

SHIRLEY. What ain't you dwelling on, Jake? *(moving past him to the couch)*

JAKE. *(to* **SHIRLEY***)* These punks in Chicago…they robbed me. I come inta that room – and there they was – on either side a the door, so I says, "Hi," though in my gut the boat is rockin', cause it was Friday – payday. And – bam – right in the middle a my "Hi," I get this leg of a chair splittin' over my skull. *(He laughs at the memory.)* My rooming house pals! Ohhh, a second chance – another shot – that's all I want.

SHIRLEY. Is that why you come back from Chicago? Because those guys beat you up?

*(***JAKE** *takes a slug from the scotch.)*

TERRY. *(indicating a beer on the coffee table)* You said you wanted a beer, Jake.

JAKE. I do! I need it. *(coming to sit beside* **TERRY** *on the couch, where* **TERRY** *and* **SHIRLEY** *have settled)* Ta…kill the rotten rich-bitch taste. A couple a drinks a that scotch and I know – I mean, I know – exactly who I ain't. No rich bitch!

SHIRLEY. I had this rich guy pick me up last week across the river…and he had lots of bucks, because he had this car, it was like made in Europe somewhere. A real money guy. So we get to his place and he says ta me, "You gotta pinch me first." And I says, "I what?" "Pinch me," he says. "Just to get me goin'." I says, "You got rocks for brains, Mister."

TERRY. Why did he want you to do that?

JAKE. Where'd he want you to pinch him?

SHIRLEY. *(as* **TERRY** *and* **JAKE** *study her)* It's embarrassing to say. His titties. So he starts givin' me "Please, please…" "Get outa here," I tell him. "Go play in the traffic." He was not my cup of tea. Honest ta God.

*(***TERRY** *stands and, agitated, moves near the piano.)*

TERRY. I gotta ask you something.

SHIRLEY. Okay.

TERRY. Whata you doin'?

SHIRLEY. Whata you mean?

TERRY. You know what I mean. She knows what I mean. Whata you think you're doing? What's so hard about that?

SHIRLEY. Terry, c'mon, whata you askin' me?

TERRY. I mean, for god's sake, it's obvious, isn't it? I mean, you're not pretending you don't know what I'm asking you.

SHIRLEY. I don't. Honest.

TERRY. Crime-ah-nittlee! I almost married you.

*(The door opens and **DANNY** and **KAREN** enter. **DANNY**'s tie is off, his shirt open at the collar, his jacket loose. **KAREN** is bundled in her jacket, her arms folded across her stomach, hugging herself. Clearly they were expecting an empty house.)*

JAKE. Hey, Dan!

DANNY. What are you guys doin' here?

TERRY. We got worried about you, man.

JAKE. Yeah, you disappeared.

DANNY. Pop and Benji kept cartin' us around until they went into the tavern and we could walk home.

TERRY. That's where they are – over the tavern sloppin' up hooch? Those two guys are beautiful, you know that? Together all the time. All the time.

SHIRLEY. Hi, Danny.

DANNY. Hi, Shirley.

KAREN. I'm Karen.

DANNY. This is Karen. Karen, I'd like you to meet Shirley, and –

JAKE. And I'm Jake. *(moving to **KAREN**)* We sort of saw each other on the run but we were not formally introduced.

TERRY. Danny, who you think put the match to the hill? BUNCHA GODDAMN KIDS!

JAKE. He's Terry.

TERRY. I'm Terry!

JAKE. How was your dinner?

KAREN. *(as she sits on a kitchen chair)* Great.

JAKE. What'd you have?

KAREN. Roast beef and mashed potatoes.

JAKE. Ohh, my favorites. How'd that suit go over, Dan? You get a lot of compliments on it. That's my ole man's suit he's wearing.

KAREN. I'm cold. I'm freezing. Is anybody else cold?

DANNY. You want my jacket.

JAKE. You mean, does she want my dad's jacket.

KAREN. Ohhh, my teeth are going to be chattering.

DANNY. I'll get you a blanket. *(worried about her)* What's going on do you think?

*(As **DANNY** heads upstairs for a blanket, **JAKE** sits down near **KAREN** at the table. He pours her a scotch.)*

KAREN. When I had pneumonia, I was eight and I felt like this…all awful. *(She drinks in a gulp and shudders.)* Eecccccgggg! I kept dreaming about automobiles banging into one another.

JAKE. Yeah? I bet your dreams are very interesting.

KAREN. The cars didn't bend though, and get crooked and like out of shape. They melted into each other.

JAKE. Neato.

KAREN. It was revolting. *(looking curiously at him)* Hi, Jake, hi…! Hi…!

JAKE. Hi.

KAREN. Hi, hi…I got some dope, you want some?

JAKE. Whatayou mean?

KAREN. Some pot.

TERRY. *(to **DANNY** who is coming down with a blanket)* Hey, Danny, didn't it make you feel weird to have the hill burnin' and we didn't do it?

DANNY. Man, I thought you probably lit it.

TERRY. I wish I had done it. I wish I had started it.

KAREN. *(As* **DANNY** *guides* **KAREN** *to the couch, she roots in her purse.)* We're gonna have a little pot, right? If I can find it.

DANNY. No, no, no.

KAREN. It'll be good. It makes people very mellow, Danny. Everybody just forgets about their differences. *(sitting and still rooting)*

JAKE. That sounds scary.

DANNY. Jake, she's done enough – I don't want her doin' any –

JAKE. It ain't my idea.

KAREN. Here it is. *(producing the joint)* Got a match?

(She is nestled on the couch in the blanket. **JAKE** *approaches with his lighter.)*

JAKE. Dan, this could be good, don't you think – us all gettin' together. Losin' track of our differences. *(lighting the joint, which* **KAREN** *has at the ready)*

TERRY. Sounds great to me.

*(***KAREN** *takes a drag.)*

KAREN. Here's the deal, though? *(giving the joint to* **JAKE***)* I'll share my wonderful grass…with you if you promise that you will all leave in fifteen minutes, so Danny and I can be alone.

SHIRLEY. I promise.

JAKE. How about in twenty minutes? *(passing the joint to* **TERRY***)*

DANNY. Twenty sounds good. Fifteen sounds better.

TERRY. You want us here, don't you Dan? We're his friends. *(inhaling smoke, then passing the joint)* This is weird. You feel anything?

JAKE. *(settling onto the floor near the piano)* I got so much alcohol in me, a truck could run over me and I wouldn't know it.

KAREN. So I hear you guys are going to push some dorks around tomorrow.

JAKE. Oh, yeah? Where'd you hear that?

TERRY. Jake has dorkaphobia.

SHIRLEY. Dorkaphobia – that's when you feel certain dorks are stealing all your clothes.

JAKE. No, no, it's when your friends all start talking like dorks.

KAREN. Do you know Danny isn't going to be able to help you push these particular dorks around?

DANNY. *(beside her on the couch)* Karen, mind your own business.

KAREN. You're going to have to push these dorks on your own because he's going on a picnic with my mom and dad and me.

DANNY. I never said that.

KAREN. You just don't know it yet.

JAKE. *(leaning in)* What's the deal, here, Dan? We're countin' on you.

DANNY. I told you I wasn't going on the picnic. *(then to JAKE)* I told her.

KAREN. But to no avail. I'm warning you. I have my ways.

JAKE. I'm gonna put on some music. Let's put on some music. *(moving to the record player)*

DANNY. How you doin', Karen? You okay? You warm enough.

KAREN. Actually, I'm hot. *(flinging blankets off)*

DANNY. *(as he tries to tuck her in)* No, no, no, no. Stay wrapped up, okay. You don't know –

KAREN. God! *(getting rid of the blanket, taking off her jacket)* Will, you stop! Don't be such a fussbudget, okay? Everybody says it about me, she looks like Bambi but she's got the constitution of King Kong.

(The music comes on: Elvis Presley. And **KAREN** *gets up.)*

Dance with me, Danny. C'mon. Please. *(tugging at him)*

TERRY. *(hollering at the sky)* I'm drunk as a skunk and there ain't – !

KAREN. *(spinning, arms spread)* Wheeee…! Wheeee…!

TERRY. – nothin' drunker than a – *(turning to **KAREN**)* – Shhhhhhh! – *(to the ceiling again)* – skunk. Don't know what he's doin'! *(to **DANNY**, **JAKE**)* Jesus, I'm talkin' and she's goin' "Wheeeee…!"

(**KAREN** *spins back to* **DANNY** *on the couch*)

KAREN. Did you miss me? I bet you did.

SHIRLEY. Wanna dance, Terry?

TERRY. What? No.

(**SHIRLEY** *approaches him*)

I never forgot about you, Shirley, do you know that? Never.

(She moves close and they slow dance.)

It's like The Invaders From Mars.

SHIRLEY. What is?

(as the music switches to Love Me Tender*)*

TERRY. What happened to you. That's what. God. Whata you think! And the invaders from Mars have come down and put this goddamn screw thing in the back of your neck and from then on, you are what you are now.

SHIRLEY. I'm just me.

TERRY. But you're not. And the fact that you in fact think you are, when you're not, is proof.

SHIRLEY. Boy, are you whacky.

TERRY. Shut up.

(He kisses her, then reaches and finds a kitchen chair, where he sits, she straddles him, and they neck.)

JAKE. *(eyeing them)* Look at that. Is it young love or old love or just I'm horny, you horny?

KAREN. Which do you think it is, Danny?

*(Moving close, **DANNY** and **KAREN** kiss and **JAKE** looks at them, then at **TERRY** and **SHIRLEY** kissing.)*

---

*See Music Use Note on page 3

JAKE. Hey, you guys. What's goin' on here? I'm feelin' a little left out. But that's all right. My friends are makin' out. I'm happy for you.

(For a moment, the music plays; **KAREN** *and* **DANNY** *neck,* **TERRY** *and* **SHIRLEY** *neck, and* **JAKE** *watches.)*

TERRY. *(parting slowly from* **SHIRLEY***)* Oh, that poor little frog, that poor little guy.

JAKE. What?

TERRY. *(rising slowly, moving to the kitchen table in a marijuana vision)* Oh, man, that bull snake you brought in here, Jake – it was the one. You dropped him on the table and I didn't recognize him, but he killed that poor little frog. Oh, man, you're just this poor little frog sittin' by a pond, croakin', and catchin' flies and all of a sudden – the jaws of this big bull snake close down on you. You don't even see it comin', and it's worse than dying, you're going to be eaten. And you can feel it pulling at you, and you know your deadly enemy has got you, and then above you is this other creature, this gigantic other creature and he's looking down at you, and you think he's going to save you, so you keep looking up and hoping. Oh, god, he wanted me to save him, that poor little froggy. I tole you about this, remember?

TERRY. He wanted me to save him, but I was scared.

KAREN. That was a real frog?

TERRY. Weren't you listening?

DANNY. We were all listening.

TERRY. I'm sorry, Froggy. I'm sorry. I shoulda done something.

JAKE. Terry, can you get it under control? You're embarrassing yourself.

TERRY. He was terrified. His life was over. You know what I mean, Dan?

DANNY. Sure.

TERRY. And it's happenin' right this second. Little frogs are getting eaten by snakes, and rabbits are dyin' in the teeth of foxes, and cats are eating birds, and frogs are devouring bugs and birds are sucking up bugs. It's a nightmare out there.

JAKE. Ter, you gotta knock it off about the little animals. They're okay.

TERRY. Are you nuts, Jake? Think about it. How can you not think about it?

JAKE. I don't know. I never had a problem until right now.

DANNY. *(gazing off)* What's Elvis going to die from, do you think?

JAKE. What? What are you talking about?

DANNY. Elvis.

JAKE. Why're you saying this?

DANNY. *(in a stoned, almost benign state)* He's going to die.

SHIRLEY. Elvis?

DANNY. Yes.

JAKE. Whatsamatter with him? Is something the matter with him? Did I miss something on the news?

DANNY. No. No, I mean, someday. He has to. How do you think it will happen?

JAKE. This is dumb. I don't like this. He's the king.

DANNY. James Dean died.

JAKE. Now you're being ridiculous. James Dean was an asshole. He was a miserable jerk. Of course he died. He was totally unfunloving, but Elvis – Elvis – Elvis ain't gonna die.

DANNY. *(still calm)* Of course he is.

JAKE. He's fine. He's very healthy.

DANNY. It don't matter.

JAKE. He knows how to have fun. He's a very happy guy. *(grabbing and displaying an album with Elvis' face on it)* Happy-go-lucky guy. That's all he does – is have fun – he sings songs and gets laid – he don't have a worry in the world.

DANNY. He's still going to die. It's gotta happen to him. I wonder what will happen to him?

JAKE. Why are you talking this way about Elvis?

DANNY. He's a human being!

JAKE. It ain't gonna happen.

DANNY. He's got that voice – he opens his mouth and out it comes. He can't help himself. The most beautiful voice in the world.

JAKE. That's what I'm sayin'.

DANNY. *(still calm)* But it doesn't mean he's going to live forever and sing forever. You see my point?

JAKE. No.

DANNY. How can you not see my point, Jake? Somethin' sometime has got to happen to Elvis. He can't just –

JAKE. Please! Just Listen! Shut up and listen! *(pause)* It's really beautiful. Just…listen.

(And now they all listen, each gazing into his own response to Elvis's voice, which is beautiful. This goes on for some twenty seconds, and then **KAREN** *stirs, opens her eyes, sits up.)*

KAREN. *(amazed, hushed, beginning in a kind of duet with Elvis)* Oh my goodness. It's not kicking a football, Danny – that's not what you want! What you were doing – what you felt. It was like Zen. It is Zen – chop wood, carry water. That's what you want. The feeling you described, kicking the football, being absorbed in an action, over and over, the submersion of the self – that's what you're sensing – surrender to –

(Rooting in her purse for Franny and Zooey.*)*

Listen. Listen. At the end of *Franny and Zooey* there's a secret they have to learn for the sake of…everything. *(reading)* "And don't you know – listen to me, now – don't you know who that Fat Lady really is?…Ah, buddy. Ah, buddy. It's Christ Himself. Christ Himself, buddy." That's what Zooey's explaining to Franny and that's what he tells her she has to realize. We all do.

(She takes in **JAKE**, **TERRY**, *and* **SHIRLEY**, *who gaze at her, strangely mesmerized and motionless, head in*

hands, or munching something slowly, as they were left by Elvis' song.)

– we all have to – we have to WAKE UP.

(then back to **DANNY***)* That's what they're all talking about. Ginsberg and Salinger and Kerouac and John Clellon Holmes and Mailer. And Watts! Alan Watts. There's a new age, this wonderful angel is like rising up for all to see, because we're at this juncture! They're ushering it in. "Holy, holy, holy," says Ginsberg. "The world is holy. *(Her palm pressing* **DANNY***'s heart.)* The soul is holy. *(touching his bare arm)* The skin is holy. *(touching gently his nose)* The nose is holy." "Men are afraid to forget their own minds." That's Kerouac. They're announcing it – this…this need of the soul…this opportunity… *(Again her hand goes over his heart.)* …of the soul…and we can take it or miss it… *(moving toward* **TERRY** *and* **SHIRLEY** *at the kitchen table)* …because the years will roll by and suddenly it will be nineteen eighty-four – that's what Orwell means. That's his warning. Nineteen eighty-four will be too late. Twenty years is what we have, or our chance will be gone. The world of Orwell will have arrived…and it'll be *(moving back to* **DANNY***, her sense of dread at what might come growing)* nineteen eighty-four and nineteen eighty-five, eighty-six, eighty-seven, eighty-eight…it'll be this darkness that looks like light because that's how it's disguised – a barbarism disguised as progress, a dungeon called freedom. Death will have taken over – perfectly disguised, and Big Brother will be watching – he'll be watching our every move, and we'll be afraid without knowing why, even though we know he's watching, and when he's not watching us, we'll be watching him, and we'll all be talking Newspeak – words that don't mean what they mean…and we'll be lost and…*(in distress to* **DANNY***)* Ohh, what if all that happens? – what if we don't wake up? – what if we don't even see our last chance?

DANNY. That's a lot of time. *(hoping to console her)* We'd all be in our forties in nineteen eighty-four. I mean, that's a lot of time.

KAREN. I know, but –

DANNY. People can figure things out in twenty years.

KAREN. Do you think they will?

DANNY. Think how long that is.

TERRY. I can't. I'll never be forty.

JAKE. Who's Big Brother?

DANNY. People are smart. They're really smart. A lot of things can happen in twenty years. People have common sense, you know.

KAREN. I hope so. I really hope so.

JAKE. *(easing close to* **DANNY***)* But who's this Big Brother? – that's what I want to know.

DANNY. I have no idea. But she says he'll be watchin'.

TERRY. You mean like now – he'd be watchin' us?

SHIRLEY. This once…my…husband Eddie was watchin' me…and he says ta me, "If you look at me one more time with that look, you're gonna be pickin' your teeth up for a month of Sundays." "What look?" I says. "You're doin' it again," he tells me.

DANNY. When Eddie drove his car into that tree, the whole hillside burned, didn't it.

SHIRLEY. The gas went all over everything. He had a full tank.

DANNY. Acres and acres. The car like exploded.

TERRY. How'd you feel, Shirley?

SHIRLEY. Well, I didn't feel good. Lemme tell you that.

DANNY. Everybody came out to look.

*(***DANNY*** follows a thread of thought here.)*

People like fires.

TERRY. Like tonight.

DANNY. What is it they like?

(On the trail of an idea that will link to what **KAREN** *said, he moves to* **TERRY** *in the kitchen.)*

When we used to light the hill on fire, why did we do it?

TERRY. It was scary fun if it got out of control.

DANNY. I mean, in history, too. Think about it. The things people have burned.

JAKE. *(following* **DANNY** *into the kitchen)* Like what?

(On the kitchen table, munchies have been spread – bread and peanut butter.)

DANNY. *(getting closer and closer to the idea he's after)* I'm talking about deliberately.

KAREN. Rome. They burned Rome.

DANNY. *(following into the kitchen)* People like to burn things.

JAKE. The trash.

TERRY. The hill. Somebody burned the hill tonight, we don't know who.

SHIRLEY. Atlanta. At least in *Gone with the Wind.*

DANNY. No. They really did that.

SHIRLEY. And before our very eyes this very night – poor old lady Trunkle's house.

KAREN. Nagasaki.

DANNY. Hiroshima.

JAKE. *(after a momentary pause)* The toast.

TERRY. Hamburgers.

SHIRLEY. Their fingers.

DANNY. Dresden. They burned the Reichstag. All those books.

SHIRLEY. Marshmallows.

KAREN. Birthday cakes.

TERRY. You mean candles.

(Again, they stall for a instant.)

KAREN. Witches, witches.

TERRY. Right. Witches.

SHIRLEY. Incense.

JAKE. The trash.

DANNY. And now everybody's got the bomb. Or at least us and the Russians.

TERRY. Whata temptation!

DANNY. You know that movie, *Beau Geste* – where those kids burn that little sailboat in the beginning. With the toy corpses in it. They light it on fire and shove it out into the pond.

(KAREN wanders to the couch and settles.)

TERRY. One of them plays taps on this little bugle. *(blowing taps in his hands)*

DANNY. And then later, when those three kids are men. They're still friends. And they're in the Foreign Legion.

TERRY. It's a great movie.

DANNY. Two of them are dead, except the one guy, it's Gary Cooper, he's the only one alive when this big battle in the desert's over. Both his friends are dead. He lights the fort on fire. He gives them a Viking funeral, because he loves them. He burns the fort, he burns his dead friends. I'd like to do that for you guys, you know? Somehow.

TERRY. Except we ain't dead, Dan.

DANNY. If we were on the boat now – the whole bunch of us, just as we are, we could sail like this forever. We'd just float along. It woulda been beautiful on that boat, man.

KAREN. What boat are you talking about? Is it in his books?

JAKE. No. Captain Danny here had us in training to sail away – what a bunch of clowns we were – maybe twelve, thirteen, the three of us puttin' up sheets and clothes lines and poles, man, so we could learn how to do it.

TERRY. Mainmast – mizzenmast, prow, bow –

JAKE. Mainsail, topsail, jib, square rig.

DANNY. God! We could still do it! I mean, why not? We all actually have money now. I mean it. We could do it. Get a boat, sail down to New Orleans, to the Mardi Gras.

KAREN. You're stoned.

DANNY. I'm talking about everybody here. I'm not excludin' anybody, I'm really not, Pop and Benji at the wheel, Karen and Shirley in the galley, Ter and Jake puttin' out all the sails – *(climbing up on a chair and pointing out into the future)* – and me way up in the crow's nest, pointin' the way.

KAREN. You're really stoned, Danny.

DANNY. I gotta go pee. But I ain't droppin' this when I get back. *(getting down he heads for the stairs)* I'm pickin' right up where I left off.

SHIRLEY. Can't wait.

(They all giggle.)

KAREN. He's really stoned.

JAKE. *(watching **DANNY** climb the stairs)* He looks great, though, don't he? I mean, a large part of the nice impression he makes is due to that suit. *(crossing to sit beside **KAREN** on the couch)* It was handmade in Atlantic City, New Jersey. My mom and ole man were out there on a sightseeing tour for union members at Finnegan's, and there was this tailor they came across who took measurements of every part of my dad's body so he could make the suit fit exactly at a very good price.

KAREN. We all liked it.

JAKE. What'd your folks have to say about it? I bet they were very impressed.

KAREN. Danny was the only one who had a gripe about it.

JAKE. Whata you mean? He had a gripe?

KAREN. Well, he – he wished he had his own suit.

JAKE. *(stunned)* You mean he wished it out loud? You mean he was knocking my dad's suit? He was complaining?

KAREN. Not exactly. He was just –

*(as **DANNY** comes out of the bathroom, **JAKE** looks up at him)*

JAKE. Were you or were you not complaining about my dad's suit to the rich bitch?

DANNY. No.

JAKE. She just said it. *(back to* **KAREN***)* Were you lying to me? Trying to start trouble!

DANNY. *(on the stairs)* Jake. C'mon. I tole her it wasn't mine – it was your dad's.

JAKE. *(at the foot of the stairs)* Which I suppose makes it automatically inferior. So what's wrong with it? Huh? Tell me!

DANNY. It doesn't fit.

JAKE. So get out of it!

DANNY. With pleasure.

(Tossing the jacket to **JAKE**, **DANNY** *goes up to grab pants out of the dresser.)*

JAKE. Whata night you musta had, Dan, huh, slurpin' martoonis and tearin' down your friends.

DANNY. *(stepping into* **POP**'s *room with the pants)* You're a broken record, Jake.

JAKE. Karen likes me.

(Passing behind **KAREN**, *he pours beer on her.)*

KAREN. Awwww…! Ohhhhh!

(Jumping up, only to have **JAKE** *splash more beer on the front of her dress.)*

Danny…! Ohh…!

SHIRLEY. I saw that. Jake, I –

JAKE. Shut up, Shirley, before I sit on your face.

SHIRLEY. Now look what you've done, you've ruined her dress.

KAREN. And it's pretty, too.

JAKE. Get your ex-fiance outa here, Ter?

TERRY. Don't call her that.

JAKE. Just tell her to go out and wait in the car.

SHIRLEY. I don't wanna go wait in the car. I'm going up to the lady's room. I gotta pee.

*(***SHIRLEY** *stomps up to the bathroom, as* **DANNY** *comes out of* **POP**'s *room.)*

JAKE. So what was it, huh, the suit wasn't dorky enough for you?

KAREN. *(By the sink, she starts to remove her stained dress.)* Dorkaphobia, that's when you're sure dorks are being mean to your clothes.

JAKE. You're always talkin' about you wanna take over the Blue Note, and I'll be the bouncer, and Ter'll be some bullshit –

TERRY. The bartender!

JAKE. But deep down, all you really want is to marry this rich bitch and drive an Oldsmobile and stick your nose up in the air.

DANNY. *(coming down the steps)* You don't hear me! You never hear me! I ain't gonna rot in this one-horse town planted in some stupid job with a wife and a bunch of screaming kids! I gotta get outta here.

TERRY. *(moving in on **DANNY**)* Why, though, why? You gotta tell me why. This is a nice town. We got a nice town fulla nice people, doing nice things. Why are you always thinking you gotta leave? Nice people, happy people. I don't wanna ever leave.

DANNY. Terry. Listen. What if we joined the service? Army or Navy. The three of us.

TERRY. Are you nuts – joinin' the Army? Man, I'm scared of the draft.

JAKE. The officers are a bunch of college assholes, and the sergeants are all colored guys or hillbillies. So is that what you want, three years of assholes of every possible kind tellin' you what to do?

*(As **KAREN** is hanging her dress on the stair railing. Wearing a slip, she passes behind the couch.)*

KAREN. I say no, no, to the Army for you, Danny. There's a war coming in Indo – Indo-something – China.

TERRY. *(seeing her for the first time)* Look at her. She's in her underwear.

KAREN. Dorks have poured beer all over my Bonwit Teller dress.

DANNY. What happened, Karen?

*(As **KAREN** approaches **DANNY** on the couch, **TERRY** drifts into the kitchen.)*

KAREN. I don't want to say, but I wish your friends would leave.

(She flops onto the couch.)

JAKE. Are you tellin' us to go? Is that what you're –

*(In the kitchen, **TERRY** drops his beer and picking it up, bangs his head on the table.)*

TERRY. Awwww…awww… *(falling onto the floor)* I hurt my head.

JAKE. C'mon, Ter. Let's get the hell outa here. We know when we ain't wanted. *(lifting **TERRY**)*

TERRY. What?

JAKE. Time to get off the premises.

TERRY. Good night, Danny…ole stupid Danny, Danny, Danny.

*(**TERRY** is about to go to **DANNY**, but **JAKE** pulls him back.)*

JAKE. Terry, wake up. The rich bitch ordered us out and our so-called friend stood by with his thumb up his ass.

DANNY. Give it a rest, Jake.

JAKE. This goddamn uppity attitude! That's all you got time for. Nothing's good enough for you.

DANNY. Go home, Jake.

JAKE. "Go home, Jake." *(mocking)* You sound henpecked and pussy-whipped already. You're a treacherous sonofabitch.

TERRY. Wha's goin' on?

JAKE. He didn't have to start goin' with her, but he did, and since he started, we ain't neither one a us once double-dated with him. Not once! *(to **DANNY**)* You ain't gonna be there for us tomorrow, are you.

TERRY. He didn't say that, did you, Danny?

JAKE. He don't have to say it. I can see it in his eyes. He's gonna stick it to us and go off on that damn picnic...

*(As **JAKE** moves behind the couch toward **KAREN**, **DANNY** rises.)*

...with little miss money bags here, this whore with her dope and her paradin' around in her underwear.

*(Leaning over the couch, he grabs at **KAREN**.)*

You're trash.

*(**DANNY** grabs **JAKE** and flings him sideways onto the floor where he bounces, grunts, then rolls over, looking up at **DANNY**.)*

We're gonna wake up one a these days and find you up on Citadel Avenue lookin' down on us like the rest of the greedy pricks.

DANNY. You go near her again I'm gonna kill you.

JAKE. You make me laugh.

DANNY. Yeah?

*(As **DANNY** steps toward **JAKE**, **TERRY** lunges in front of **DANNY**, stopping him.)*

TERRY. Just stop it. You're like the animals, you gotta eat each other. You gotta bite and kill and eat each other. The hell with you. *(staggering toward the door)* I'm gonna take the car and drive it into a tree!

*(**TERRY** lunges out the door.)*

JAKE. Should I let him drive the car into a tree? Would you even care. *(getting to his feet)* You're ashamed of us, man, why don't you just admit it.

DANNY. Whatever you say.

JAKE. You're an asshole. That's what I say. I eat so much shit and my ears start to drip, my brain feels brown, I'm done.

DANNY. Good. Then get out. Because I'm done, too. I'm sicka you, Jake.

JAKE. At last the truth. *(gathering his dad's suit)* So God bless Danny Mueller, may he rot in peace!

(JAKE *goes out the door. Behind* **DANNY**, **KAREN**, *on the couch, raises her hand.*)

KAREN. Danny. Can you help me a little?

DANNY. What? Yes.

(She is struggling to stand and he hurries to her, as she is coming around the couch.)

KAREN. I gotta get to the bathroom. I'm sick, a little sick. Get me to the bathroom.

(With her hand over her mouth, ready to throw up, she hurries to the stairs, with **DANNY** *right with her.)*

(on the stairs) Whoaaaa…ohhh, lemme sit. *(as he helps her sit)* There. Okay. We can go. *(starting to stand)* Uppps, no we can't. I'm so mad I did this.

DANNY. It's okay.

KAREN. Is it? Oh, you're so patient. Here we go.

(Together they go, getting her up the stairs. She flees into the bathroom, shutting the door.)

DANNY. Are you okay? Be okay.

(And then the door opens and **SHIRLEY** *comes out.)*

SHIRLEY. What's goin' on? Oh my goodness heck. *(looking around)* I fell asleep. Where is everybody?

DANNY. They took off.

SHIRLEY. Terry even? Shoot. Why'd they do that? Shoot. How could this happen? *(glancing into the bathroom)* How's she doin'? Bombed, huh? *(starting down)* Smashed and throwin' up, but still a heartbreaker. Can I use the phone? I need a cab.

DANNY. *(following)* I thought you and Terry would be in love forever.

SHIRLEY. Did you? Wow.

DANNY. Let me ask you something. I wanna ask you something.

SHIRLEY. Sure.

DANNY. It's very important. It's very, very important.

SHIRLEY. Don't get mad at me. You sound like you're getting mad. *(At the phone, she dials.)*

DANNY. I ain't mad. I just want to ask you something, and it's kinda hard to put into words but –

SHIRLEY. *(into the phone)* Hello. I need a cab please, lickety-split, okay? – it's on Raymond... *(looking to* **DANNY***)*

DANNY. Nineteen fifteen.

SHIRLEY. Nineteen fifteen Raymond, okay – lickety-split.

(Grabbing a nearby Coke, she takes a big drink.)

DANNY. Was it ever special, Shirley? That's what I want to know.

SHIRLEY. I am really thirsty. I'm gonna have another Coke, okay?

DANNY. *(following her to the fridge)* This is important. I want it to be special with Karen. What can I do for her? What makes it special?

SHIRLEY. *(searching the room)* Have you seen my shoes? *(heading for the couch)* I gotta have my shoes and the cab's gonna get here. *(Seeing her shoes under the couch, she bends, gets them.)* Ooops, got 'em. It's a slippery slope – then it's a rocky road. *(sitting to put them on)*

DANNY. What can I do to make it special for Karen, Shirley? I want it to be special. You gotta tell me, was it ever special for you? Do you remember?

SHIRLEY. Was what ever special?

DANNY. I thought that for a girl it was special.

SHIRLEY. What was?

DANNY. Shirley. C'monnnn!

SHIRLEY. You c'monnnn.

DANNY. *(as* **SHIRLEY** *starts for the door)* I don't know who else to ask.

SHIRLEY. *(turning on him, sticking out the empty Coke bottle)* Kookie, Kookie, lend me your comb. You're kookie, Danny, asking me that. *(Marching to the door, she turns and scolds him.)* You shouldn't be so kookie. Nobody likes it.

*(***SHIRLEY*** goes, closing the door on him.)*

DANNY. That's it. I'm done! I'm sick of it! Everybody always hiding everything.

(KAREN emerges from the bathroom, brushing her teeth.)

It's all this big goddamn secret. I don't want to do it anymore.

KAREN. I'm borrowing somebody's toothbrush.

DANNY. My mom used to make me rice pudding! And I loved it. She would make me bread pudding and rice pudding and I love them both. *(hurrying to the piano)* She would play silly songs on the piano when Pop wasn't around. We sang along. She played sad songs, too, sorrowful ones sometimes, just for the two of us. I would come home from school and she'd have bread pudding or rice pudding waiting. *(He scans his surroundings.)* It's all hers. She picked it all out. The wallpaper and the curtains, the pictures even, the rug and the couch. *(touching the couch)* We had to have it reupholstered, but... *(moving back into the kitchen)* But then one day, she was just layin' there. Still warm, but kind of frozen. It was right here. *(jumping, stomping both feet)* I found her. I come home. I knew she was sick, but nobody warned me. She'd been gonna throw out some garbage when she keeled over. It was all around her. Egg shells and coffee grounds – this Cheerios box and greasy wax paper in a ball, and this feeling, like a hole with nothing in it. I tried to clean up the mess. Like that would fix things. Like there was something to fix. It coulda been her ghost – this need, need, need. Pop took me and sat me down at the table. I was only ten, and he told me stuff. But I knew better. I knew that if somethin' so crazy could happen I wasn't really so good as I wanted to be, as I thought I was or hoped to be – so important or strong. I was like the egg shell... scattered and just nothin'.

(He looks up to KAREN, who leans against the bannister at the top of the stairs.)

KAREN. Did you ever think of killing yourself, Danny?
DANNY. What?

KAREN. Have you?

DANNY. Why?

KAREN. You mean why am I asking? Or why would you do it?

DANNY. It's kind of amazing, that's all.

KAREN. What is?

DANNY. That you'd ask.

KAREN. I must think of it every day.

DANNY. *(climbing toward her)* I wouldn't want anybody to know, though.

KAREN. That's so smart.

DANNY. You think so?

KAREN. Fool them. Why let them in on it? They'd all just pretend to care, anyway, especially the ones who didn't give a damn.

DANNY. I'd go up in the park, the cliffs at the quarry there – those cliffs must be as high as a football field is long. That's where I'd go. I'd have a letter with me. I'd be readin' this letter that I'd let slip through the fence. *(The banister seems to be the fence he gestures through, as if losing the letter.)* Then I'd climb over to get it back. *(climbing over the banister)* Anybody around, I'd say, "I gotta get my letter." Once I got to the edge, I'd trip like and yell.

(He lunges, leaning out, almost mid-air, holding to the rail with one hand behind him.)

Everybody would say, "Poor ole Dan got killed in an accident. Fell off a cliff."

(He looks up at her and they meet eyes for a charged second, before he spins and climbs down the outside of the stairs to the floor.)

You know, when I'm reading *Catcher in the Rye*, the way I told you.

(He hurries to the closet under the stairs and grabs the book, then moves to the couch.)

DANNY. *(cont.)* I can't get over the way he says all these things that I think. I can't believe this guy actually wrote 'em down.

*(Searching pages, as **KAREN** joins him, and they sit looking together.)*

But I read and they're right there. And there's this one page in particular. Things I never say to anybody. Sometimes, I swear, they're things I don't even know I think them until I read them. It's making me have some crazy thoughts. Really crazy. That maybe I could try to be a writer, too. Pretty crazy, huh?

KAREN. Why is it crazy?

DANNY. I mean, I got all this stuff in my head all the time and it's weird. Maybe I could do something with all that if I was a writer, and not just hide it.

KAREN. Danny, you could.

DANNY. But how? *(flopping back on the right side of the couch)* I mean, I'm here in the middle of nowhere.

KAREN. We're all in the middle of nowhere somewhere, Danny. *(She flops to the other side.)* We're all just these little bodies, you know. Do you ever think that? I do. And some of us are big or little relative to each other. Or relative to a dog or cat or bug, and at this second, you and I are these bodies in this room, and if the ceiling came off, it would all be so big, the sky, the stars, and we would be here talking and thinking about where we are and what we want to do and have happen, and all the while we're just these little bodies – just these sad and tender little bodies, these frail and fragile little bitty bodies.

DANNY. Millions and millions…all over the world at this second. And I'm one.

KAREN. And I'm one.

*(Their hands search for and find each other and they kiss. As the kiss ends and another might begin, **DANNY** realizes where he is.)*

DANNY. I got a bed. This is my bed.

(He bounds up and starts to turn the Castro into the bed.)

KAREN. What, what? *(seeing what he's doing)* Oh, okay.

(The bed flops down and they stand on either side of it, moving slowly toward each other. And then they kneel on the bed, and he enfolds her in his arms.)

DANNY. Ohh, man. I never felt anything like this. Never. What is this? I feel like crying. *(taking her head between his hands)* Who are you?

KAREN. Little me in the middle of nowhere.

(They kiss at length and part.)

DANNY. One spooky…girl.

KAREN. And you're the boy from the bus stop. *(pulling off his tie)*

DANNY. What if I hadn't been there? I almost wasn't.

KAREN. But you were. We were.

(They kiss again, but he breaks it off.)

DANNY. The bus could of gone. It could have taken you off. *(laying her down on the bed)* No, no. You can't do it. You can't leave. When do you go back East? You can't go back.

KAREN. It's okay.

DANNY. What day? What day? I won't let you.

KAREN. I have to. It's school. Tuesday.

(She kisses him; it goes on and then he pulls back.)

DANNY. Tuesday? No, no. That's too soon. That's not possible.

(He kisses her longingly, trying to possess her with the kiss, to keep her. And then he has a solution.)

I'll come with you. I hate this town. Where is it again? East, I know. But –

KAREN. Shhhhhhh, Danny, shhhhhh.

DANNY. Is it a secret?

KAREN. No, it's not a secret. But you can't come out there.

DANNY. But I can. *(kissing her neck, her breasts)* I can. I can. I can.

KAREN. Not right now.

DANNY. Of course I can. *(kneeling, tugging off her pantyhose)* There's trains, planes, cars – Or I could hitchhike.

KAREN. But it wouldn't be a good idea. *(rising to her knees)* There's something I'm caught up in – and it's very entangled, I need time to – because he's a teacher, actually.

DANNY. A teacher?

KAREN. But I'm going to get away from him. I am done with him.

DANNY. Okay, okay. There's somebody. There had to be somebody. You're too beautiful for there not to be somebody. But you're done with him, and I'm here. I'm right here.

KAREN. I wanted to tell you – I tried to tell you.

DANNY. *(taking hold of her)* I love you, Karen. I love you. I swear to god.

KAREN. Say it hurts in your heart. Say the love hurts in your heart. *(clinging to him)* I love you so much my heart feels like its gonna jump out of me. I want to rip it out, that's how much it hurts.

DANNY. What did you just say?

KAREN. That I love you. That I'm done with him and –

DANNY. No, not that.

KAREN. Danny….what?

DANNY. Wait. Shhhhh. I feel like there's somebody else here. *(startled, almost stricken, looking around)* I feel like it's her. My mom, my mom – that she's here. That she came in. But she can't be, can she?

KAREN. Oh, Danny. No. I don't think so.

DANNY. Why not? Why can't she? If she did, if she visited, where would she want to be? *(looking around)* Would she want to be…there…at the piano?

(He moves to the piano, touching it, caressing it, then looking back at **KAREN**.*)*

DANNY. I know it can't be true, but it feels maybe…you know…maybe.

KAREN. *(moving to him)* Danny.

(As she enfolds him in her arms, he sinks, feeling weak.)

DANNY. Oh boy, oh boy.

For a moment they are huddled together. Then there is laughter off, **POP** *and* **BENJI** *approaching, merrily.* **DANNY** *and* **KAREN** *panic, trying to grab clothes, but there is no time and she dives back in the bed, under the covers, while* **DANNY** *bounds over the bed to the other side.* **POP** *and* **BENJI** *come in, laughing about something. Then* **POP** *surveys the mess his house has been left in.*

POP. Oh, look Benji. Such a mess. They set off a bomb, these poor children.

BENJI. *(teasing)* Danny, you okay? You don't look okay.

POP. Such a mess. Danny, Danny, Ohh, what do I care? Danach kraeht kein Hahn. *(No cock crows for this.)* Let's have scotch, Benji.

BENJI. *(Seeing the scotch on the table, he hands it to* **POP**.*)* Danach kraeht kein Hahn.

POP. They have left a little of my wonderful scotch.

BENJI. No more scotch for you, Danny.

*(***BENJI** *moves in on* **DANNY**, *still teasing, and then drifting behind the couch.)*

POP. Where is Karen? Gone, I would imagine. Fleeing such disorder.

BENJI. *(having noticed the lump under the sheets)* I think she's hidin'.

POP. What?

BENJI. Somebody's hidin'. In the bed.

POP. *(delighted)* Oh, oh, it's probably that terrible Shirley.

(BENJI moves around the bed and POP approaches DANNY directly, mischievously.)

Ready or not –

DANNY. – Benji, no! –

POP. – Achtung, fertig, los! *(On your marks, get set, go!)*

DANNY. Pop, don't.

BENJI. *(lifting the sheet off KAREN)* Bingo!

POP. Uh, ohhh. Uh, ohhhhh. *(even more delighted)* Danny, Danny. What is this, Benji? What do we say now?

BENJI. It ain't Shirley.

KAREN. *(Scrambling up, she darts to the stairs, grabbing her dress off the bannister on her way up to the bathroom.)* You're ridiculous, the both of you. I don't know what you are saying.

(She goes in, slamming the door.)

POP. She scolds us, Benji. Shall we cower? I am afraid. Are you afraid?

DANNY. Pop. Please. Stop.

POP. Stop what? Life? *(enjoying DANNY's distress)* Look at him, he does not know what to think.

DANNY. Something strange…is happening to me.

POP. Of course. Always. This strange life. It happens. It comes at us. It walks up, it walks away. Like that girl. Up the stairs. Gone. *(handed a shot of scotch poured by BENJI)* This life, our life. It is a trick show. *(He toasts the trick show and drinks.)*

DANNY. I thought mom was here.

POP. You what?

DANNY. Mom was here. I know she was.

POP. Your mama? Do you hear Benji? He tells us he thought his dead mama was here. *(advancing on DANNY)* No, no. Sorry to say. But no, she is with the dead of the earth, the dead of the world, the piles of millions in ashes and dirt as the fire has left them. *(tapping DANNY's head)* Maybe in here. But not in the world. No, no. No, no. You do not tell such lies. *(fierce now)* She would come to you, not me, her husband? Liar! Her spirit would visit you, her foolish child, and leave me alone?

DANNY. Yeah, she would. *(standing to face **POP**)* We had secrets, Mom and me... Things we did together you never knew about and you never will. Because what are you, but hot air? *(walking over bed to the piano)* All you do is shoot your mouth off. *(opening piano lid with a bang)* Every word.

POP. Danny, what are you doing?

DANNY. *(pounding the piano)* You brag and brag, about –

POP. Stop.

DANNY. – how tough you were, how you stood up to the Nazis –

*(The shouts and discordant notes bring **KAREN** from the bathroom. She has her dress on.)*

POP. – You stop –

DANNY. – I don't believe you did any of it – *(discordant chords)* – and all you were back there is what you are now – a blowhard. That's what the men in the bar call you.

POP. Stop it. Stop –

DANNY. – and Brown laughs behind your back – you and your dimwit partner actin' –

*(**POP** slaps **DANNY** in the face. He strikes **DANNY** hard in the shoulder, and **DANNY** moves to walk away, but **POP** seizes him, will not let him walk away.)*

POP. No. You do not talk that way to me. It is forbidden.

*(**DANNY** erupts, grabbing **POP**, shoving him backward until **POP** goes over onto the bed, where he immediately tries to rise, and **DANNY** shoves him down again, with a loud howl. **DANNY** straightens, looming over **POP**, warning him to say down.)*

DANNY. No more.

(DANNY, aware suddenly of KAREN looking down, moves for the door, gathering her purse, her shoes, and jacket from the floor. On the bed, POP sits up, watching as KAREN hurries down to DANNY and they go out the door.)

(Silence. BENJI is unmoving. POP stands slowly. He begins to straighten the piano, closing the lid, returning the stool to its place as he speaks.)

POP. I walk around, Benji. I pick up a book. I sweep the floor. I drink my coffee. Little tears run from my eyes. I don't know why. They will not tell me. They hide their reasons. They are mine, but they are out of the sky.

BENJI. Don't be sad.

POP. But I am. Why say don't be?

BENJI. I don't know.

POP. It is good to remember. It is good to be sad. When a man is sad, he is a man. Men are sad. I am a man. Why should I be ashamed? No, no. You are wrong.

BENJI. Okay.

(POP looks up at the top of the stairs, and then his body remembers and traces KAREN's flight down and away.)

POP. He runs away with his Karen – she flees down the stairs. I cannot help it. I wish to be young.

(Weary, weakened, he needs to sit down, making his way to the edge of the bed.)

They are a wind that whirls, these young. Ein Wirbelwind. It sweeps us away. Do you not feel it? Do you not hate them a little? *(sitting on the edge of the bed)* If only in a way you barely can peek to see, deep in the heart. A cold little turning in the stomach. Is it fear? Am I not a ghost as I sit here, Benji?

BENJI. The folks'll be lookin' for me, I think. I'm gonna go home.

(BENJI goes. POP is alone.)

(blackout and music: a harsh fall of guitar.)

SCENE 2

(Morning. **POP** *sleeps on the pullout bed. Silence in the bright light of day streaming in. A breath of quiet and then the door opens and* **BENJI** *comes in. He carries a package wrapped in brown paper and tied with string. It is fresh from the post office.)*

BENJI. Emile, Emile. *(startled to find* **POP** *in the bed asleep, he lowers his voice)* Emile…

(He hurries to the bed and shakes the box to make it rattle.)

We got it.

POP. *(almost groaning)* What? What?

BENJI. The chess. The chess. It come. *(hurrying to the kitchen table)* I got it. *(grabbing scissors from the drawer)* We got it!

POP. Benji, wait, wait! Benji, stop!

BENJI. *(Having cut the string, he tears the paper off the box.)* It's the chess. I wanna see 'em.

POP. We will. *(as he sits up, wobbly)* But wait. Wait.

BENJI. *(Seeing* **POP**'s *condition, he walks over to give* **POP** *the boxed chess set.)* Want some aspirin? I got some.

POP. Oh, thank you.

BENJI. Boy oh boy, is it hot. *(Hurrying back to the kitchen, he takes a bottle of aspirin from his pocket.)* When I washed dishes in that hole-in-the-wall cafe, it was hotter than Hades. *(Pouring ice water into a glass, he shakes aspirin into his palm.)* The oven was hot and the grill and the hot water was hot. And you gotta stay clean around food – sweat drippin' out my elbows.

POP. *(Having opened the box, he holds a chess piece.)* Plastic. I should have known – paid all that money for plastic.

BENJI. *(hurrying over)* I think they look good.

POP. *(as* **BENJI** *hands him the water and aspirin)* I got to stop thinking so much, Benji, and just have fun. I say to stop. But I don't do it.

BENJI. *(pointing into the box)* I like the horse one.

POP. Benji, we must make the arrangements. Like we do for checkers. Set up the table. *(moving to the kitchen table, holding up the knight)* Yes, the horse one. The knight. In Karl's hands it behaved like a creature alive. Leaping in a L. Checkmate! And the enemy king must cringe and plead.

*(***BENJI** *is busy closing the bed, moving beer bottles from the coffee table to the end table beside the couch.)*

BENJI. You're a real bully, ain't you. But my king ain't gonna cringe and all that. We was butchers, too.

*(***BENJI** *places the coffee table so the end points to the couch. As he picks up the piano stool, which he will make his chair, he uses it as a flamethrower to tell his story.)*

My Uncle Wilbur, the Marine – he was the flamethrower fella – and he killed forty-six little yellow Japs, lined up and burned 'em alive.

POP. *(approaching with a kitchen chair and the chess box on the seat)* Chess is very hard, Benji. You must understand that.

BENJI. Okay.

(They sit across from each other, the table and chess between them.)

POP. Not every person can learn. In my excitement I may have built up too big a dream. You may not be able to learn.

BENJI. I bet I can.

POP. *(taking a book from the box)* Well, we have this little book that I ordered. It's for beginners. Now Benji, what I want you to do is –

(As he hands the book to **BENJI**, *the door opens and* **DANNY** *comes in.)*

BENJI. Hey, Danny. Our chess come.

*(***DANNY** *walks to the kitchen table where he sets down a blue duffle bag, a paper bag, and a smallish notebook.)*

POP. Danny. Hello. Good morning.

(**DANNY** *climbs the stairs without a word.*)

BENJI. And I got a book.

(**DANNY** *goes into the bathroom.* **POP** *stares up at where* **DANNY** *has gone. Then he shifts, stands.*)

POP. Benji, we cannot do this now.

BENJI. *(deeply engrossed in the book)* What?

(*As* **DANNY** *comes out of the bathroom and starts down,* **POP** *moves to the base of the stairs.*)

POP. Danny. I want to talk to you. Are you all right?

(*Passing him,* **DANNY** *goes to the kitchen table and* **POP** *follows.*)

DANNY. Whata you think?

BENJI. *(barely looking up at* **POP**) Let's get playin'.

POP. *(stepping and gesturing to* **BENJI**) No. Benji, I told you we can't do this now. Please. Thank you. *(back to* **DANNY** *at the table)* Danny. Did you get Karen home safely?

DANNY. Whata you care? *(dumping tooth paste, a brush, a razor from the paper bag)*

POP. Why do you say that? I should not have slapped you. I was wrong – I admit it. I apologize.

DANNY. That's got nothing to do with anything.

POP. Of course it does. You're a grown man.

DANNY. No. You're so fulla shit. You're all so fulla shit. I took her home, but I wish I hadn't. Her parents were nuts. Screamin' at her, screamin' at me. I wandered around all night, sittin' and drinkin' coffee, and walkin' and thinkin' until I could call this morning, and her mom and dad both got on, blowin' their tops that Karen never wanted to see me again. So I went up – right up to their house – I knocked on the door. Her dad came and he said he was callin' the cops. Then he said she was gone already. They'd taken her to her uncle's.

POP. Oh, Danny, I'm sorry.

DANNY. I don't know what I'm gonna do. *(back to packing the items on the table into the duffle bag)* But I gotta do something.

POP. Sit. We will talk.

DANNY. No. I'm not ten years old anymore, where you sit me down at the table and tell me what to think and what to feel.

POP. Of course not.

*(He sits as **DANNY** can barely stay still.)*

But it's good to sit with your father. For hours we discussed the plan for my life, my father and I. My two elder brothers, one a butcher, one a farmer. "You, Emile," he said to me, "you will be a scholar." When I say –

DANNY. I can't do this. I don't have time. *(grabbing bread, peanut butter to make a sandwich)*

POP. But we must.

DANNY. No. I gotta get movin' and pack. There's a two o'clock train and I'm takin' it.

POP. What? You're taking a train, Danny? You cannot mean today.

DANNY. There's nothin' more to say about it.

POP. But where are you going? For how long? Danny, why would you go so sudden?

DANNY. I'm gonna find Karen. She's gonna be in Philadelphia. I gotta talk face to face. I gotta see the look in her eyes.

*(He walks away to the closet under the stairs, leaving **POP** bewildered.)*

BENJI. Emile, I got 'em all right now. Every one in their right little squares. And it ain't been –

*(**POP** cannot believe **BENJI** is still there.)*

POP. *(turning to look at **BENJI**)* What are you doing here? I told you to go home. *(rising, walking to **BENJI**)*

BENJI. *(having set up the chess men according to the book)* But I got 'em all ready and I see how the knight goes in a L and –

(As BENJI moves the knight in an L pattern, POP slaps BENJI's hand, knocking the piece loose.)

POP. Stop!

BENJI. That hurt.

POP. Can you do one little thing? Can you put our stupid plastic junk back in the box? *(as BENJI gapes at POP)* What do you stare at? I must talk to Danny. Do it. Or is that too hard?

BENJI. Don't holler!

POP. *Du Hohlkopp. Du Clown.* Away! Away!

(He knocks the chess flying.)

BENJI. *(standing)* Look what you done!

POP. Get out. You do as I say. Get out! *(pointing at the door)*

BENJI. Stop hollerin'.

POP. I will holler if I want!

BENJI. Not at me, not – *(retreating behind the couch toward the door)*

POP. At you – at anybody I want –

BENJI. – not at me. Not at me –

POP. I tell you to go, you go! NOW! OUT! OUT, OUT!

(BENJI goes and POP shuts the door. He stands, his back to DANNY, who has returned to the kitchen. After beat, POP turns around to face DANNY.)

So we will be men. No more little boy at the table. We will have some schnapps. Yes? What do you say? *(moving to grab the schnapps bottle and two glasses, which he puts on the kitchen table)*

DANNY. I gotta pack.

(DANNY moves to the closet, taking the duffle with him, throwing an old, battered suitcase onto the couch, as POP approaches. DANNY has clothes from the closet, which he puts into the suitcase.)

POP. *(urgent, knowing* **DANNY** *will soon be gone)* What is it? These things! You tell me your mama visits you, not me, – your dead mama, and I fill with fury. No, no, first I am hurt. It happens like lightning. Lightning, lightning and more lightning – I am hurt – I feel lost. Let us consider. Father and son.

(Talk of the ghost of his mother has stopped **DANNY**. *He sits on the piano stool, attending* **POP** *who sits across the coffee table from him, his desire to understand, to explain, even stronger.)*

We are men in a room in a house, and Annelie is a ghost. We fight about a ghost. It is true what I say. Why would I do that? What do I lose to a ghost? Is it not already gone? If she gave me so much, why do I not have it? Where could it be? And Karen. You feel lost. She will not talk to you. Her parents forbid it and she surrenders. You think there is love. Where is it?

(Rising, he goes to the kitchen table, where he pours the schnapps into two glasses.)

Let me tell you about Karen. *(as* **DANNY** *stands)* Her little German face, I think. How sweet. She is a skull and bones like the rest of us.

DANNY. What? *(moving toward* **POP***)*

POP. I mean no harm, Danny. I mean only what is it, this life we live? Who are they, these others who tear at us? Annelie the ghost you say came to you? Did she rush through the room? Did she touch you and flee? How did you know? Have the schnapps.

(He offers the shot glass to **DANNY** *who takes it and drinks. And* **POP** *drinks.)*

DANNY. Something…ripped at me. I felt ripped open.

POP. Annalie, Karen – one dead, the other – where? Our heads, our hearts, Danny. They fling us about. Now you will be cast in the wake of this girl, this Karen. What if you find her and she does not care to see you? What then?

DANNY. Then I'll know.

(He turns and goes back to the closet, his suitcase. Left at the table, **POP** *notices the notebook* **DANNY** *brought in when he arrived. It still lies there, and* **POP** *picks it up, opens it, stands reading for a few seconds as* **DANNY** *is distracted, packing, and then he glances up, sees what* **POP** *is doing.)*

DANNY. Hey. Put that down.

(He races over, grabs the notebook from **POP.** *)*

POP. I'm sorry, but it lay here and –

DANNY. It's private. *(tossing it into the duffle bag)*

POP. I started to read and – Let me see. Or you read it to me.

DANNY. No. No.

(But he stops; he walks back, grabs the notebook from the bag and, pacing, starts to read.)

"I stood looking at her house – they wouldn't let me in – and all of a sudden, I felt like she was never real. None of it – the whole night a phantasm. Just another of my daydreams like the Blue Note Bar or that stupid boat. *(He takes a breath.)* But then I remembered – we lay on the couch and she spoke of the sky and she spoke of our smallness, our little bodies in the big world, and I felt ripped open. My mom's spirit came to me. It was in her. In Karen, and she brought it to me. Karen gave my mom's soul back to me."

(beat)

It's what I'm gonna try to do.

POP. You keep a journal? I didn't know you were doing such a –

DANNY. I don't know what it is. Wandering around. Up all night – I just started. My head was gonna explode and it made sense for me. A kind of sense.

POP. It's well done, Danny. Yes, yes. You misspell a word here and there –

DANNY. I don't give a damn how they're spelled. *(tossing the notebook into the duffle)*

POP. But if someone reads it, they will think you are ignorant. You must go back to college.

DANNY. I can't keep talkin', Pop. There's nothin' more to discuss.

(He walks around the couch, grabbing his work boots. He sits on the piano stool, putting them on.)

POP. In my beloved German I make my meaning – mich perfekt ausdruecken. *(approaching with a hunger to be understood)* In English I am an ape with a stick. Once on our Rotherbaum Street – I tell the truth to you, Danny – you must know this! I made my protest in high German. I shouted my warning; I was brave, I was principled, but I deterred nothing. My words were no more than the sunshine – the warm summer rain through which the devils walked wearing their big smiles. In the next week, Annalie and I were warned we must run. We fled down the stairs. Though I did not intend my life, I chose it. Now I am here. And so you choose yours.

DANNY. *(a beat before he looks at his watch)* I gotta hurry, Pop.

(DANNY rises and walks past POP and hurries up the stairs.)

I can't miss this bus. If I miss the bus, I'll miss the train.

(DANNY rushes into the bathroom. POP stands, looking up. Then he turns and walks toward the door. He takes his hat from the hook and goes out, quietly, leaving the door open. After a beat, DANNY hurries out of the bathroom, carrying a towel, a washcloth.)

I'll write you a letter, as soon as I –

(Failing to see POP, he stops. He looks around, searching, as he descends the steps. And slowly he realizes that POP is no longer there, leaving him dismayed for an instant. But he has little time. He puts the towel and washcloth into the blue duffle, zips it shut, then checks

that the snaps on the suitcase are secure. He picks up both bags and stands, looking over the empty rooms, as if to imprint them in his memory. Music begins, the piano introduction to "Can't Help Falling in Love."* **DANNY** *raises the blue duffle over his shoulder and, with the suitcase in his other hand, he turns to go in a pathway of light that seems a kind of fire, as Elvis sings and* **DANNY** *goes out the door. He passes the window and is gone, as the pathway slowly fades.)*

(blackout)

---

* Please see Music Use Note on Page 3.

Available From Samuel French

David Rabe's

The Basic Trainging of Pavlo Hummel

The Black Monk

The Dog Problem

Goose and Tomtom

Hurlyburly

In the Boom Boom Room

The Orphan

Sticks and Bones

Streamers

Those the River Keeps

www.ingramcontent.com/pod-product-compliance
Lightning Source LLC
Chambersburg PA
CBHW071410290426
44108CB00014B/1764